OREGON'S GOLDEN YEARS

OREGON'S GOLDEN YEARS

Bonanza of the West

By

MILES F. POTTER

THE CAXTON PRINTERS, LTD.
Caldwell, Idaho
1987

First printing July, 1976
Second printing March, 1977
Third printing December, 1978
Fourth printing January, 1982
Fifth printing November, 1987

© 1976 by
The CAXTON PRINTERS, Ltd.
Caldwell, Idaho

Library of Congress Cataloging in Publication Data

Potter, Miles F   1895-
    Oregon's golden years.

    Bibliography: p.
    Includes index.
    1. Oregon—Gold discoveries.   2. Gold mines and
mining—Oregon.   I. Title.
F880.P67   979.5'04   75-12292
ISBN 0-87004-254-8

Lithographed and bound in the United States of America

148554

FOR MY FAMILY

CONTENTS

Page

FOREWORD ix

ACKNOWLEDGMENTS xi

1. SHINY PEBBLES IN THE CREEK 3

2. STRIKES IN THE SOUTH 13

3. STUMP TOWN TALE OF GOLD 32

4. AUBURN WAS OUT AHEAD 39

5. OUTFITTERS FOR THE MINES 42

6. DESTINY RIDES THE GOLD BOOM 49

7. BIG STRIKE IN WHISKEY GULCH 61

8. TIGER TOWN AND OTHER CAMPS 69

9. FORTUNE HUNTERS INVADE THE MOUNTAINS 78

10. THE SAGA OF GREENHORN 81

11. WHEN THE MINERS DANCED 90

12. QUEEN CITY OF THE MINES 95

13. THE VIRTUE DIGGINGS 104

14. BONANZAS BY THE DOZENS 109

15. GOLDEN SUMPTER 116

16. SUMPTER'S WONDERFUL NARROW-GAUGE 129

17. MOTHER LODE OF THE BLUES 138

18. LAWTON AND ALAMO LIVED BRIEFLY 148

19. COPIA'S HORN OF PLENTY 152

20. BOOM AND BUST 158

21. GOLD BLAZED THE WAY 168

NOTES AND BIBLIOGRAPHY 171

BIBLIOGRAPHY 173

INDEX 178

FOREWORD

THE DISCOVERY OF GOLD in California in 1848-49 and in southern Oregon in 1850-51 came at a time when the Oregon Territory consisted of what is now the states of Oregon, Washington, Idaho, and parts of Wyoming and Montana. This vast land contained only 9,083 settlers, most of them in the Willamette Valley.

There were few roads and almost no money. A bushel of wheat was the medium of exchange. Mail came occasionally by ocean steamer, but not on a regular schedule. There were no markets for crops. The land route to the settlers' former homes was the Oregon Trail, across two thousand miles of wasteland inhabited by Indians. This isolation from friends and relatives, plus the hardships, were only part of the troubles endured by our hardy forefathers. As the decades widen the distance from frontier times, we are inclined to dismiss them as having been highly romanticized. Perhaps these words will serve as a reminder, "Lest We Forget."

The discovery of gold helped usher in a new era. Markets were stimulated, bringing in money to pay for much-needed goods. Roads, stages, steamboats, all forms of transportation and communication followed in the wake of discoveries, first in southern Oregon and then in the area east of the Cascade Mountains. When the Donation Act and the Homestead Act were passed by Congress, the farmer and the merchant quickly took advantage of new opportunities.

The stampede to the goldfields was launched. Thousands of men with only a pick, shovel, gold pan, and grubstake took off into the wilderness, a rich land where no man had ever stuck a plow. The miners would soon need supplies, and the wise merchants and farmers found themselves with a captive market and a supply of gold dust to pay for the things they had to sell. Along the trails and roads leading to the mines, overnight stops were established. Soon these places became towns, and, with the arrival of a post office, each acquired a name, often the one given by the first settler.

People pushed on. New roads were built, new towns sprang up everywhere. By the time the gold rush was over and the mines had slowed down, more stable industries had been established. The same steamers that carried miners up the Columbia returned downriver loaded with wheat, a new kind of gold. They carried to market thousands of head of livestock and millions of pounds of wool — "white gold." In time, wagons, stages, and steamboats surrendered to the railroad. Thousands rode the train instead of the prairie schooner across the continent to the "Promised Land." Oceangoing ships carried lumber, wheat, livestock, wool, fruit, and newly manufactured Oregon products to all ports of the world.

Again, it was the discovery of gold at the right time that furnished the stimulus needed for the growth and economy of

Oregon — as well as the entire area west of the Rocky Mountains. Gold from Western mines helped to win the Civil War.

The early importance of gold to this region is emphasized by the pick incorporated with other symbols of her industries on the Great Seal of the State of Oregon, serving as a reminder of the role the precious metal played in the development of the Oregon Country and the Pacific Northwest.

MILES F. POTTER
Portland, Oregon

ACKNOWLEDGMENTS

THE WRITER, a member of the third generation, asked an old-timer approaching the end of the trail, "How long have you lived in this country?" In a squeaky voice and with a twinkle in his eye, he said, "Sonny, I been in these parts since a year before the sagebrush was planted."

It has taken five years of research to compile this story of man and his lust for gold. The facts have been gleaned from the mouths of men, recorded history, steamboat and stagecoach records, newspapers yellowed with age, picture collections of museums and pioneer families (some glass-plate negatives used to produce the pictures are well over a hundred years old), bank deposit slips, mining claim recordings hidden away in county courthouses, old assay certificates, and visitations to long-forgotten mining camps.

I am indebted to many people for their documents and newspapers, faded with age, and for the reminiscences of pioneers and county officials who helped willingly to remove the dust from files of old-time mining records. My thanks go to the museums in Canyon City and Jacksonville, to the Oregon State Department of Geology and Mineral Industries, to the Oregon Historical Society, to Harold McCall, Oregon City photographer, who traveled and worked with me throughout the state reproducing the old-time pictures, to Mr. and Mrs. Orville Fleetwood for their research, to Otis Ford, the so-called Mayor of Granite, for his amusing stories, to the family of pioneer Daniel W. Elliott for much information, and to Arthur Woodwell of Sumpter, Oregon, the best and last of the old-time assayers. (Arthur doesn't talk much, but what he says can be depended upon.) The individual who was most helpful was the late O. H. P. McCord of Baker, Oregon, a well-known eastern Oregon historian. Many of his pictures and a wealth of material gathered over a period of eighty years are incorporated in this book.

MILES F. POTTER
Portland, Oregon

OREGON'S GOLDEN YEARS

SHINY PEBBLES IN THE CREEK

ADVENTURES TO STAGGER THE IMAGINA-TION were experienced by early miners as they traversed the wilderness in their search for gold. People traveling through Oregon today on broad highways, railroads, and airplanes have faint conception of the hardships endured by their forefathers. After crossing the plains in covered wagons, encountering untold dangers, early miners moved into a vast primitive area inhabited only by Indians. This didn't dampen their enthusiasm. Gold drew miners and would-be miners like a magnet — and just as rapidly. A single strike (or even a rumor) could turn an area topsy-turvy. A single poke full of nuggets started a gold rush that helped to settle all the Oregon Country east of the Cascade Mountains, and the story has become a legend.

It happened when a group of pioneers on their way to the Willamette Valley decided to take a shortcut from Idaho. Now known as the "lost wagon train of 1845," these hardy souls unknowingly changed the course of history. This was the beginning of Oregon's "Golden Years." It also had a tremendous effect on the entire Pacific Northwest and, to some degree, even on California.

The tide of emigrants to the Oregon Country started in the years 1842 to 1845. Only 137 persons made the 2,000-mile trip in 1842, but next year the number increased to 875. In 1844 there were 475, but by 1845 there were 2,000 — and this group brought 7,500 head of cattle. By 1852, 18,000 people had made the crossing to their new home in the West.[1] It was a gigantic land, so even this steady migration settled the region only sparsely — and nearly all the early pioneers were heading for the Willamette Valley.

One large party hired Stephen Meek, older brother of Joe Meek, to guide them across the plains.[2] For some unknown reason his services were terminated at Fort Hall on the Snake River, in what later became Idaho.

It had been a long, hard journey. By the time the first group of wagons stopped at Fort Hall, the train was strung out for many miles. There seems to have been wide-spread disagreement among its members, and some wagon captains were relieved of their commands. After a brief rest, those in the lead continued for 300 miles along the Snake River to Fort Boise, built by the Hudson's Bay Company in 1834 and located where the Boise River flows into the Snake.[3] They arrived late in August. On this part of the journey they were not guided by Stephen Meek; he and his wife, accompanied by a man named Nathan Olney, traveled alone.

At Fort Boise, however, Meek met again with some members of the wagon train. He told them of a shorter route to the Willamette Valley that would save from 150 to 200 miles. There would be less danger from the Indians, he said, and, while no wagons had even been over the shortcut, the trails had been used for years by both Indians and members of the Hudson's Bay Company.

Courtesy Oregon Historical Society

Stephen H. Meek was the older brother of Oregon's famous Joe Meek and was the man responsible for the Lost Wagontrain of 1845.

He was familiar with the country, he added, having trapped over most of the area.

Meek drew a map outlining the route he would take. Here the first confusion shows up. At least one diary records that Meek said they were to go up the Malheur River and down the John Day to the Columbia.[4] Others say they were to follow the Malheur and then take the ridges west to the Deschutes and Crooked rivers, then north to The Dalles. Over the years, writers and historians have tried to outline the actual route taken by Meek.[5] Most agree that the party traveled far south of the John Day River, yet there is some evidence that they did reach the river.

In any case, most of the wagon train decided to follow Meek. The final decision was made when they stopped to rest at a hot springs near where the town of Vale stands today. The owners of fifty wagons decided to continue along the Oregon Trail. But over a thousand people, with some 200 wagons

Courtesy Oregon Historical Society

Fort Hall was established by Nathaniel Wyeth, an American in 1834, and located in what is now Southeastern Idaho on the Snake River. It was a fur traders' post but was not successful. The Hudsons Bay Company purchased the Fort, equipment and stock in 1836 for $8,179.94. The stock consisted of gaudy blankets, fancy butcher knives, tobacco, coffee, powder, lead, looking glasses and alcohol — all attractive to the Indians.

Courtesy Oregon Historical Society

Old Fort Boise was established in 1834 by the Hudsons Bay Company on an island where the Boise River flows into the Snake River, 300 miles northwest of Fort Hall.

The tide of immigrants crossing the plains to Oregon increased to 2,000 by 1845. By the time the first group of wagons rolled to a stop at Fort Hall, the train was strung out for many miles.

and 2,000 cattle, horses, and mules, voted to take the cutoff.

History in gold was made that day, August 25, 1845, when the large party of pioneers left the established trail and headed up the Malheur River where no wagon had traveled before. This group was to suffer hardships and many deaths before the first tattered remnants started trickling into The Dalles in October.

They followed the Malheur for about twenty miles, over terrain almost impassable for wagons. Some broke down, causing delays while repairs were made. A few wagons were left behind. One diary states, "You could follow the steps of the weary oxen by the traces of blood in their tracks."

The first person to die was a babe in arms, Emaline McNemee. The infant was carried three days before a suitable burial place could be found. The second death was that of Sarah Chambers. She was buried beside the rocky trail. After each burial the wagons passed over the graves to hide them from the Indians. No accurate record exists of the number who died; historians estimate there were at least twenty-three — possibly more.

Many stops were made to rest and to repair equipment. One stop was supposed to have been made near the headwaters of the Malheur River, on a clear stream running in a southwesterly direction.[6] One story relates that the women took the occasion to do some laundry along the banks. Children playing beside their mothers noticed

Gold nuggets like these were found by members of the lost wagon train. Unfamiliar with raw gold, they called them pretty little golden pebbles; most were cast aside as worthless.

"shiny golden pebbles" in the water and in the grass along the water's edge.

Another family believes the location was on Canyon Creek, near present-day Canyon City. George H. Himes, pioneer and curator of the Oregon Historical Society, has written[7] that William F. Helm said his father, mother, five brothers, one sister, and himself were members of the Meek party. Helm stated that his family's wagons and camp utensils, including buckets, were painted blue. They were camped on a tributary of the John Day, Bill Helm said, when the small yellow pebbles were found along the water's edge. Nobody realized it was gold. James Terwilliger and Thomas R. Cornelius supported Helm's story that the golden pebbles were gathered in an old blue bucket and left behind when the wagon train moved on. This is the beginning of the oft-told legend of the "Lost Blue Bucket Mine."

These people for the most part were farmers from the Midwest and East, with no idea of the appearance of raw gold. We must also keep in mind that this was three years before the discovery of gold in California. Believing the pebbles worthless, the pioneers tossed most of them aside; however, a few found their way into tool boxes. Had it not been for the few nuggets saved, the story might have been forgotten. So far as is known, this was the first gold discovered west of the Rockies by a citizen of the United States. Hubert Howe Bancroft, Western historian, recorded: "The first gold discovery in Oregon made by an American, if not by any person, was made near the headwaters of the Malheur River by what is known as the 'Lost Wagon Train' in the year 1845."[8]

The following men are said to have seen and examined the golden pebbles: Mr. Herren, Solomon Tetherow, Will Helm, Isaac Simpson, W. G. T'Vault, John Durbin, Thomas R. Cornelius, James Terwilliger, Sanford Patch, H. D. Martin, and

The *Oregon Spectator* published at Oregon City in 1846 was the first newspaper on the Pacific coast. The editor was W. G. T'Vault.

Theophilus Powell. There are few today who doubt the authenticity of this gold discovery. The integrity of the witnesses is a substantiating factor:

William G. T'Vault became editor of the *Oregon Spectator* published in Oregon City, the first newspaper on the Pacific Coast. Later he became postmaster general of the provincial government and a member of the territorial legislature.

James Terwilliger was well known in Portland. He constructed the town's first frame building for his blacksmith shop at First and Morrison. Terwilliger Boulevard is named for him.

Thomas R. Cornelius served twenty years in the state legislature and was named a colonel during the Indian Wars. The town of Cornelius is named for him.

Don Herren and Isaac Simpson became successful farmers. William Helm was a Methodist minister, as was Theophilus Powell.

These witnesses were all responsible and reliable men, and it would appear, therefore, that gold was found by the Meek party. However, because the mine has never been located, there has been much mystery attached to it, as with other "lost mines" of the Old West, and many articles have been written about the "Lost Blue Bucket Mine."

Historians agree generally that the Meek party swung far south of the John Day River

before turning north to make their way to The Dalles on the Columbia River. Every foot of the supposed route has been gone over with a fine-tooth comb for over 123 years.

Do the words used in the Helm diary — "glistening in the sunlight in and along a clear little stream" — describe a location that would be so hard to find if it were on the trail of the wagon train as the maps show it? Isn't it reasonable to suppose, since these people were hopelessly lost at times, that somewhere an error was made in recording their exact location?

We do know that gold was discovered later on Canyon Creek, near where Canyon City stands today — $15,000,000 worth in the first three years.[9] It was found along the banks of a clear little stream, exactly as the Helm diary described it. Is this the answer to the lost gold mine?

Mr. Helm was so sure the strike was on Canyon Creek that later, when gold was discovered (or rediscovered), he spent several years mining there. If you are still looking for the lost mine, don't look any more.

Canyon City sign reads as follows: "Gold discovered here June 8, 1862. Twenty-six million dollars in gold came from here."

In 1857 a new Fort Walla Walla was built at the site where the city of Walla Walla stands today. The town grew up around the fort. It became the county seat in 1859 and chartered as a city in 1862; 127 soldiers were stationed here to protect the Oregon Trail.

You are not only more than one hundred years too late, but $26,000,000 have been taken from that "little stream." In any case, history records it as the "Lost Blue Bucket Mine," and that's exactly what it is — wherever it may be.

Members of the Meek party were rescued eventually and continued on to the Willamette Valley. Their unheralded discovery of gold started the search for a legendary lost mine and, sixteen years later, resulted in the great rush that settled the entire area between the Cascades and the Rockies. Undoubtedly the Meek party changed the course of history.

The Indians, seeing this migration of white people into their country, soon started trouble, and for a while the Oregon Trail was almost deserted. The trouble became known as the Cayuse War, which resulted in the Whitman Massacre in 1847. Soldiers were called in 1850 to guard the emigrants. Traffic on the Oregon Trail picked up until 1855, when another uprising broke among the Indians, particularly along the Columbia River. Several tribes joined forces to rid their land of the white settlers, for by this time there were about 15,000 pioneers in the Willamette Valley.

The combined Indian tribes mustered a war party of over fifteen hundred. The bloody war lasted until 1858, when most of the Indians were placed on reservations.[10] Later events show that while this ended the collective movement of the Indians, it didn't finish the individual efforts of a few warlike chiefs who continued to kill and plunder for a number of years.

Because of a shortage of troops, General John Ellis Wool, in charge of the Department of the Pacific, issued the following order in 1856:

"No immigrant or other whites, except Hudson's Bay Company persons having ceded rights from the Indians, will be permitted to settle or remain in Indian country or on land not ceded by treaty, confirmed by the Senate and approved by the President of the United States. These orders are not however to apply to miners engaged in collecting gold. The miners will, however, be notified that should they interfere with the Indians or their squaws, they will be punished and sent from the country."[11]

This order was later rescinded, but when gold was discovered east of the Cascades in 1861 roving bands of Indians continued to murder and plunder. There were only 54 soldiers at The Dalles and 127 at Fort Walla Walla, for the Civil War had begun.[12]

With no protection, no prospective market for their produce, and no place to buy supplies, the pioneer wagons still continued westward along the Oregon Trail, bypassing the fertile valleys and timbered

The interior of a pioneer covered wagon, showing the possessions so many started the long journey with across the plains. Many times it became necessary to discard the heavy pieces along the trail in order to lighten the load.

Courtesy Oregon Historical Society

In the early 1840s before the Barlow Trail was opened to the Willamette Valley, The Dalles was known to the pioneers as the landing — the end of a 2,000 mile journey by prairie schooner. Here the wheels were taken from the wagons and the dissembled parts placed on log rafts, then floated through the dangerous Columbia rapids to the valley. Many were drowned when the rafts were pounded to pieces by the wild water.

mountains east of the Cascades. Their destination — the Promised Land of the Willamette Valley.

In the early 1840s The Dalles was known as "Wasco-Pum." To the pioneers arriving from across the plains, it was better known as "The Landing." It was only a tiny outpost, but to the weary travelers it marked the end of the long journey by wagon, although more dangers lay ahead. Wheels and other disassembled wagon parts were placed on log rafts and floated down the Columbia River to the valley. The rapids were extremely dangerous; some of the unwieldy rafts were torn apart and many people drowned — a heartbreaking ending to a long, hazardous trek across prairies and mountains from their former homeland which, even if they survived, they would never see again.

The pioneers who settled the Willamette Valley were a courageous, slow-moving people with Midwest habits. They had almost no communication with the outside world. There were no markets and few industries. The only available money was a few Spanish coins. A few personal possessions were all that the emigrants could bring on the long journey. Their clothing

was worn out and difficult to replace. Most men wore ill-fitting buckskins and the women homespun dresses of coarse local wool. There were few tools, most of them handmade. Nearly all the land had to be cleared of timber before crops could be planted. Wheat, the money crop, was reaped with scythe and cradle. Mail came to the valley by sea — from six weeks to two months old.[13]

But the country was growing. The first American post office on the Pacific Coast was located March 9, 1847 at Astoria near the mouth of the Columbia River, with J. M. Shively the first postmaster. This same month Oregon City received its post office, followed by Portland and Salem in November 1849. Stamps were not sold in Oregon until 1852. Before that, all letters were mailed collect. A charge of forty cents was made and the amount written in the upper left-hand corner of the envelope.[14]

After 2,000 miles of hardship crossing the plains and mountains, the pioneers reached the Willamette Valley, but their troubles were not over. The land had to be cleared of brush and timber before planting. Wheat, the money crop, was reaped with a scythe and cradle; there were no markets and almost no communication with the outside world.

Courtesy Oregon Historical Society

This picture portrays the inside of a cabin of long ago. Only the essential items were left after the 2,000 mile journey across the plains. Many keepsakes were discarded along the trail in order to lighten the load.

During these early days, all cooking was done over an open fireplace. In many cases handmade wooden dishes and furniture were used. With no coin or other currency, wheat soon became the medium of exchange. A bushel of wheat was valued at one dollar.

The terrible isolation became at times almost unbearable for the settlers. There was no escape. The only land route in or out was the Oregon Trail, a distance of 2,000 miles and six months' traveling time. Another problem was continual friction between the provisional government and the Hudson's Bay Company, which controlled the Columbia River and could virtually paralyze travel at the portages — for the Indians living there were obedient to the fur trading company.[15]

In 1846 the provisional government authorized Samuel Kimbrough Barlow to build a toll road which would make it possible to bypass the Columbia at The Dalles. The road was nearly straight up and down but it was usable, and the covered wagons continued to roll into the Willamette Valley.[16] However, there were times during the winter when deep snows closed the road. Jesse Applegate and his brother Lind-

say had each lost a son when their boats overturned in the Columbia River rapids, and they decided to search for a safer year-around road. They left Oregon City in 1846, traveling southward along a route where Eugene, Roseburg, and Grants Pass stand today. From Grants Pass they swung east to the Klamath Valley, fording the Lost River near Humboldt, Nevada. They then traveled northeast by way of what is now Winnemucca, Elko, and Wells, Nevada, joining the Oregon Trail near Pocatello, Idaho. As with others, they passed through land where yellow treasure lay but never came upon it.

At Fort Hall the Applegates painted such a glowing description of the new trail that one hundred wagons decided to try the route. The trip proved disastrous; over half the people perished along the way. Time and again they were attacked by Indians. The hills were so steep it took all the oxen in the train to pull a single wagon to the top. Sharp lava cut the animals' feet, and both people and stock were completely exhausted by the time they reached the Umpqua and Calapooya Mountains. When a young girl died, they buried her at the foot of an oak tree. The Indians dug up the body and hung it from the tree. This is how Graves Creek got its name.

By November 1846 the party was fighting its way down Canyon Creek. Many wagons were abandoned. Some emigrants mounted their animals, others traveled on foot. Many died of shock and exposure, and the trail was littered with abandoned wagons and personal keepsakes, which were claimed quickly by the Indians who followed the train like vultures. The trail was bitterly denounced by Governor George Abernathy; however, during the gold rush the route became known as the Applegate Trail and was extensively used.[17]

Such hardships were blood money in a gamble to reach a land claimed by Great Britain, the United States, and the Indians. At this time the two governments decided the forty-ninth parallel would be the boundary line between the two countries — but no one in Washington bothered to inform people in the Northwest that the disputed land was now part of the United States. Some time later a ship arrived with a newspaper telling of the transaction. The year 1846 faded into 1847, and still no official word of the treaty reached Oregon. No territorial governor was appointed, no laws enacted. Only silence.[18]

News of the Indian attack on November 11, 1847 at the Whitman Mission at "Waiilatpu" finally brought action. On August 14, 1848, Congress declared Oregon a territory. President Polk selected Joseph Lane of Indiana as territorial governor and mountain man Joseph L. Meek as marshal. The territory consisted of what is now Oregon, Washington, Idaho, and parts of Montana and Wyoming. In all this vast land there were only 9,083 white people — 5,410 men and 3,675 women — almost all living in the Willamette Valley or close by. Much of the territory was undeveloped wilderness occupied by Indian tribes. There were no roads, and most travel was done by water.[19]

The future for the new territory and its handful of plucky citizens looked dark. Yet at that moment an incident was happening that would alter things for all the West, and particularly the Pacific Slope: Gold was discovered in California. This opened a market for Oregon's products and gave the people gold and silver to use as media of exchange instead of wheat.

News of the gold strike came to Oregon on July 31, 1848, when the schooner *Honolulu* arrived. Usually ships came to sell goods, not to buy. But this ship arrived with nothing to sell. The captain began purchasing all the provisions, tools, picks, and

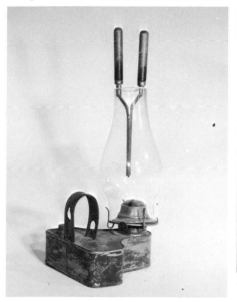

Old-time coal oil lamp. My ladies' curling iron was heated in this manner.

This home-made churn turned out many a pound of butter in its day.
Courtesy Oregon Historical Society

The lady's sad face and toil-worn hands tell a story without words.
Courtesy Oregon Historical Society

shovels that were available. It was only after the supply was exhausted that he told of the gold strike in California. Wild excitement prevailed, and soon the stampede southward began. Twenty vessels arrived at Portland loading wheat, flour, salmon, butter, eggs, shingles, lumber, and meat of any kind. Almost overnight wheat jumped from one dollar a bushel to six.[20]

Before the end of 1849 more than fifty vessels had headed south from Oregon loaded with supplies. Imported Mexican and Peruvian silver dollars were paid for the provisions. One ship, the *General Lane* from Oregon City, discharged her cargo at Sacramento. She had several tons of eggs on board. The captain sold them to a passenger for thirty cents a dozen. The purchaser peddled them in Sacramento for one dollar each.[21]

The economy of the Oregon Country boomed. Portland built a covered wharf to handle goods during the rainy season. New sawmills sprang up. An all-weather plank road was constructed to the farming communities in the Tualatin plains. Many Oregon men traveled south to the goldfields, some by ship and others overland on foot or horseback. That fall the territorial legislature could not meet for lack of a quorum.

Most Oregonians returned to their homes with from $1,000 to $5,000. Governor Lane estimated that they brought back two million dollars; another two million came to Oregon in payment for goods before the end of 1849.[22] Oregonians found they didn't need to journey to California to share in the treasure of the Sierra. It flowed north into their pockets, tills, and bank vaults for the goods Oregon could provide. Oregon fed and clothed the miners who were too busy in the creek beds to plow and plant the soil. And it wouldn't be long before the trove would move onto home soil; prospectors and miners with pick, pan, and burro were combing the draws, hills, and box canyons of Oregon's raw hinterlands in search of gold.

Lindsay
Applegate

A typical large family group in Oregon's early history. Note the Bible on the table, the organ, and the coal oil lamp.

Lindsay Applegate and his brother, Jesse, each lost a son in 1843 while rafting their wagons down the Columbia. This tragedy caused the two men to hunt for a new route. They founded what later became known as the Applegate Trail. (Jesse never wanted his picture taken; this is a poor drawing.)

STRIKES IN THE SOUTH

THE DISCOVERY OF GOLD in California developed ocean travel between Sacramento, San Francisco, Portland, and Oregon City. From the Willamette Valley, the only land route south was the trail used by the Hudson's Bay Company in their trade with the Indians of southern Oregon. Again, gold came to the rescue. This time it was in our own backyard.

In 1850 a party of prospectors working northward from California found yellow nuggets in Josephine Creek near what is now the Oregon-California border, close to the junction of the Illinois River.[23] The discovery that made the real boom in Oregon, however, was on Jackson Creek, near what is now the picturesque town of Jacksonville. In December 1851 two packers found a small nugget in the creek gravel. They told two other packers, Jim Claggage and James R. Poole, of their discovery. In January 1852 Claggage and Poole camped overnight at the spot. They uncovered abundant yellow gravel and named it Rich Gulch.

The town of Jacksonville was born in the rush that followed. At that time the boundary between the two states had not been well defined. Yreka was considered by many to be in Oregon. This made it convenient for the fortune-seekers: When the tax collector from California arrived, the miners decided they were in Oregon. By the time the Oregon collector arrived, they were loyal citizens of the Golden State. Some voted in both states.

Mail to the northern mines came overland from Sacramento. Trouble with the Indians made delivery hazardous and expensive; each mail shipment required a military escort. The government decided to set up a mail station at the mouth of the Klamath River. A group of speculators, hearing about it, decided to establish a town there. They chartered a worn-out schooner, *Samuel Roberts,* for the task. Being inexperienced seamen, they sailed beyond the mouth of the Klamath and on north to the Rogue River and Coos Bay. Probing the inland area, they decided neither route was suitable to reach the mines, so they sailed on to the mouth of the Umpqua. After talking to the Indians, they decided a suitable trail could be established over the mountains and south to the California mines.

It was here the party met Levi Scott, who had staked a land claim at the head of the tidewater. They joined forces and sailed the *Samuel Roberts* to a new townsite which they named Scottsburg. A trail was developed from Scottsburg to the new town of Winchester, located at the junction of the Hudson's Bay trail leading south. From here, they followed the old trail to the northern California mines.

The trail was completed in 1851, just in time to cash in on the gold rush near Jacksonville. At times there were as many as 500 pack animals waiting at Scottsburg for the incoming boats.[24] Within a year the Scottsburg trail widened into a road, joining the trail south from the Willamette Valley at Winchester, which was to become the first

Jack Sutten photograph *Courtesy Oregon Historical Society*

Old-time prospector with his three burros, old-timers called them Rocky Mountain Canaries

county seat of Douglas County. Long strings of horses and mules pulled heavy wagons loaded with everything from Bibles to whiskey. Frequently a barrel of whiskey was lashed close to the driver's seat and a straw inserted through a small hole. Near the point of delivery, the barrel was refilled with water from a nearby creek and the hole plugged.

The winter of 1852-53 was bad. Heavy snows blocked the trails and roads, making travel next to impossible. Supplies at the mines ran short and prices rose to a new high. Flour sold for a dollar a pound, tobacco a dollar an ounce. Salt was so short it was traded for an equal weight of gold.

Soon after the discovery of gold, Jackson became the most populous county in Oregon. People came from the Willamette Valley, California, and far away midwestern and eastern states. Production increased as new discoveries were made in Josephine and Douglas counties. Then came the Sailors Diggings near Waldo, for a time the second largest town in southern Oregon. The strike got its name from a party of sailors who deserted ship at Crescent City after hearing about the rich find at Jacksonville. Journeying across the Siskiyous, they camped on the upper Illinois River and at this point located the rich ore. It has been estimated that $4,000,000 was taken from the Waldo-Takelma area. A single nugget weighed fifteen pounds.[25] The largest nugget unearthed on the East Fork of Althouse Creek in 1859 weighed seventeen pounds

Jacksonville in 1858, the center of the southern Oregon gold rush

Peter Britt photograph

In 1850 Scottsburgh was established on the Umpqua River at the head of tidewater. Steamers from San Francisco and Portland unloaded supplies on the docks, all destined for the mines in northern California and southern Oregon. As many as 500 pack animals carried the supplies southward to the mines. Packers charged 12¢ to 30¢ a pound.

The Decker General store at Waldo built in 1863; first called Sailors Diggings. In the 1850s, living was high: flour $75 a hundred; sugar 60¢ a pound; butter 90¢ a pound; lard 80¢; eggs $1.50 a dozen; tobacco $1.00 an ounce.; cigars $120 a hundred.

Gold like this was found on or near bedrock close to the surface, and at first mined with crude placer equipment. (Dish U.S. National)

troy.[26] One must be careful when telling about large nuggets of the early days, for the old-timer was not above a bit of leg-pulling. There's the story of a miner who found a lump of gold so large he could not carry it. Afraid to leave his treasure, he sat down on it and starved to death.

The miners dug a ditch costing $75,000 to serve the Althouse and Sailors Diggings. The gravel was so rich the ditch paid for itself the first year. Many new strikes were made along the Rogue River system — Kerbyville, Williams Creek, Althouse Creek, and the Applegate River. On the headwaters of the Rogue, many camps sprang up, among them Pleasant Creek, Evans Creek, Willow Creek, Foots Creek, Starvout, Jumpoff Joe, Coyote, Graves, and Tom East Creek. Scottsburg became a thriving seaport with hotels, stores, saloons, gambling houses, and the first newspaper south of Salem — the *Umpqua Weekly Gazette,* first published in 1854.

The discovery of gold in southern Oregon came at about the time the Donation Act was passed by Congress in 1850. Under terms of the act, each resident who was a citizen of the United States (or who within a year declared his intentions of becoming one) could receive 320 acres and, if married, another 320 acres in the name of his wife. Combined with the discovery of gold, this act was the stimulus necessary for the permanent growth and development of southern Oregon. Roads were built to supply the mines, and over these roads traveled hundreds of homeseekers. Finding the desirable land in the northern valleys already taken, many traveled on to stake their claims in the rich valleys of the south. They found a climate to their liking and a ready market at the mines for their produce.

The discovery of gold ruined the Hudson's Bay Company by taking away its most trusted servants. Some sought their fortunes in mining while others, when the land laws were enacted, took the oath of allegience to the United States. Jacksonville became the center of activity, with several thousand miners coming and going — a lively place with miners and farmers mingling in the crowded streets and saloons. As usual in a mining town, the saloons did a land-office business. It was a bonanza for gamblers and camp followers.

In time tents and log cabins began to dis-

Waldo, Oregon in 1861; first county seat of Josephine County in 1856, at that date the largest town in the county. It is located southwest of Cave Junction. The white two-story building on left was the hotel and stage office. An estimated $4,000,000 in gold was taken from this area. A fifteen-pound nugget came from here.

The Esterly mine, also known as the Llano de Oro, was the largest placer mine in the Waldo area. Estimated production $600,000.

Hydraulic elevator used at the old Easterly mine to elevate water and tailings out of the pits which were worked to bedrock three to fifty feet below ground level.

appear, to be replaced by substantial buildings, and Jacksonville became the metropolis of southern Oregon. While this was going on, the farmers in the valleys were prospering, too.

Passage of the Donation Act caused the greatest flood of emigrants in history over the old Oregon Trail. From May 21 to June 5, 1850, four thousand wagons passed Fort Kearney, Nebraska, heading west. Prospects of a golden treasure at trail's end was part of the lure.

One of the first orders of business when the miners arrived was the forming of mining districts. Each district drew up a set of laws. Crime increased as the camps grew in size and number, for each village had its saloons and gamblers, and later its dancehall girls. Before organized law arrived, it often became necessary for vigilantes to restore order. They may have been short on law, but quick action at the end of a rope did help to settle things down.

By 1880, 5,438 mining claims had been filed in Jackson County. In 1855 Jacksonville got its first newspaper, the *Table Rock Sentinel*. The publisher was W. G. T'Vault, who had published the paper at Oregon City.

Jacksonville flourished — the largest city between San Francisco and Portland. The famous United States Hotel boasted a stove or fireplace in every room. President Rutherford B. Hayes slept there.

The Adams Express Company of San Francisco opened an office in Jacksonville in 1853. There were no roads leading south, so untold millions in gold moved by pack train to the mint in San Francisco. C. C. Beekman was the banker, first arriving in Jacksonville as manager of the Wells Fargo Express office, then gradually becoming involved in personal banking. His bank building still stands, purportedly the only bank in the United States that did not pay interest to depositors. He charged the depositors for keeping money there!

Today the quiet streets reveal little of the

Jacksonville showing courthouse built in 1883, now serving as the Southern Oregon Historical Museum.

A group of old-time gold miners in front of their cabin

The man with the whiskers is C. C. Beekman, old-time banker and Wells Fargo express agent during the gold rush in Jacksonville.

William G. T'Vault, at one time leader of the so-called Lost Wagontrain of 1845. Later he became editor of the *Oregon Spectator*, founded on February 5, 1846. He was the first newspaper editor on the Pacific Coast. Later he became Postmaster General, a member of the Territorial Legislature and on November 24, 1855 he established the newspaper in Jacksonville known as *The Table Rock Sentinel*.

past. No longer do they echo to the shouts of bearded miners. Nor do you see long pack trains and freight wagons unloading their heavy burdens. No longer do stagecoaches arrive and depart amidst clouds of dust, for those days are gone. Yet one may still find ghosts of the past in Jacksonville. In

Beekman's bank is an advertisement telling the arrival and departure times of the stages to Portland and California. On the counter is a pair of gold scales. In 1929 Mr. Beekman told Fred Lockley of *The Oregon Journal* that millions of dollars in gold dust were weighed on these scales and shipped to the mint in San Francisco between 1852 and 1861.

Jacksonville's City Hall, built in 1856, was once a general store. In looking over the town, someone said to an old-timer, "There must be five or six hundred people here." The old-timer shook his head. "No," he replied, "there are over 2,000, but more than

Banking office of C. C. Beekman, old-time Jacksonville banker; he paid no interest on deposits, but charged depositors for leaving money in his bank.

Front of Beekman's bank; for many years he was local agent for Wells Fargo Express company.

Millions of dollars in raw gold were weighed on these Beekman bank scales before starting its long journey to the mint in San Francisco by Wells Fargo Express.

Peter Britt and his first camera. He traveled 2,000 miles in a two-wheeled cart to Jacksonville in 1852; perhaps the first professional photographer in Oregon.

1,500 of them are in the graveyard on the hillside."

One of the best museums in Oregon is located at Jacksonville. Some of the collections are priceless. Jacksonville was the home of photographer Peter Britt, who arrived there in 1852. He owned what was perhaps the first camera in the state, brought across the plains in a two-wheeled cart. Some of his pictures are famous, including the first photographs of Crater Lake. Many can be seen in the museum, along with his camera and equipment.

Courtesy Oregon Historical Society

The southern Oregon homestead cabin of Peter Britt, one of the earliest photographers in the state

Courtesy Oregon Historical Society

The first stage line from Portland to Sacramento opened September 15, 1860, a distance of 710 miles. The company had a $90,000 a year mail contract with the U.S. Government. The trip was made in six days and seven hours. The stages used four to six horses and there were 60 relay stations. The company used 35 drivers, 28 coaches, 30 stage wagons and 500 head of horses. One-eyed Charlie Parkhurst was one of the early day stage drivers. A rough, tobacco chewing character who was on the driver's seat for 30 years. Parkhurst died in 1878. It was then they discovered the tough old stage driver was a woman. Since she had cast a ballot in 1868, she was the first woman in the United States to vote. (Oregon Historical Quarterly, Volume 35, pages 131-138, Osburn Winther.)

The first stagecoach line from Portland reached Jacksonville in 1858. In 1860 the line was stretched to Sacramento, a distance of 710 miles. The stage company received a $90,000 government contract for carrying the mail and also held the Wells Fargo contract. The trip was made in six days and seven hours. The stages had four- to six-horse hitches, with sixty relay stations along the way. The company used thirty-five drivers, twenty-eight coaches, and thirty stage wagons. Five hundred head of horses were needed for the operation. "One-eyed Charlie Parkhurst" was one of the famous early-day stage drivers — a rough, tobacco-chewing character who was on the driver's seat for thirty years. Parkhurst died in 1878. It was then discovered the tough, old stage driver was a woman. Since she cast a ballot in 1868, Charlie was the first woman in the United States to vote.[27]

The land between the Rogue and Apple-

Overland stage schedule, Sacramento to Portland; 700 miles in six days.

OVERLAND MAIL ROUTE
TO OREGON.
Through in Six Days to Portland!!

CONNECTING WITH THE DAILY STAGES

To all the Interior Mining Towns in Northern California and Southern Oregon. Ticketed through from Sacramento, through Marysville, over the Railroad to Oroville, connecting there with the

OREGON LINE OF STAGE COACHES!

To Chico, Tehama, Red Bluff, Shasta, Trinity Centre, Yreka, and in Oregon—Jacksonville, Canyonville, Roseburg, Winchester, Oakland, Eugene City, Corvallis, Albany, Salem, Oregon City, to Portland,

TRAVELERS AVOID RISK of OCEAN TRAVEL

Pass through the HEART OF OREGON—the Valleys of Rogue River, Umpqua and Willamette.

This portion of the Pacific Slope embraces the most BEAUTIFUL and attractive, as well as some of the most BOLD, GRAND and PICTURESQUE SCENERY on the Continent. The highest snow-capped mountains, (Mt. HOOD, Mt. SHASTA and others,) deepest ravines and most beautiful valleys.

Stages stop over one night at YREKA and JACKSONVILLE, for passengers to rest. Passengers will be permitted to lay over at any point, and resume their seats at pleasure, any time within one month.

FARE THROUGH, FIFTY DOLLARS.

Ticket Office at Sacramento, near the Steamboat Landing.

H. W. CORBETT & Co.,

July 20, 1866.
Proprietors Oregon Stage Line.

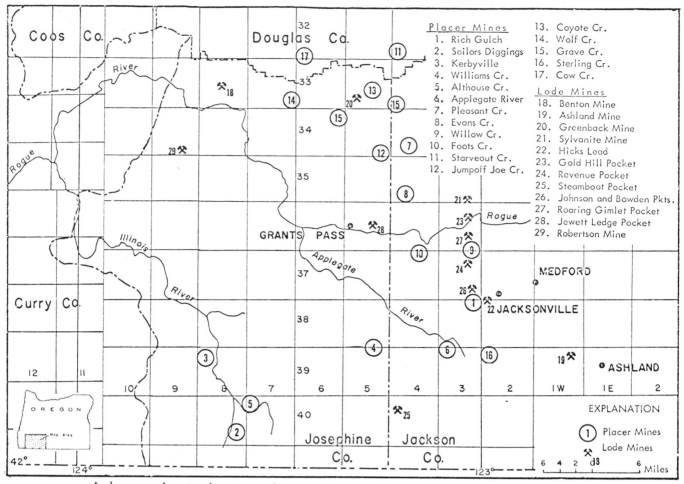

Index map showing locations of stream placer and lode gold mines in southern Oregon

gate produced a lot of gold, beginning in 1852. It was in this area that they found the famous blue gravel, which at one time was an ancient riverbed. The miners said it was "lousy" with gold but hard to extract because of a water shortage. Sterling Creek, a branch of the Little Applegate River, is the center of this rich district. Interestingly, this blue gravel was found later in eastern Oregon, where the same ancient riverbed was traced for about eighty miles.[28]

The famous Sterling Mine was at one time the largest in the state. During its best production years, $3,000,000 came from this mine. The gold came from the creek bottoms and scarred hillsides. Because of a lack of water, the mine was slow to develop. In 1877 ex-Governor David P. Thompson of Idaho took charge. The following year he completed a high ditch twenty-three miles long, seven feet wide at the top and four feet at the bottom. For the first time the mine had plenty of water.

The company installed two hydraulics, with pressure sufficient to move boulders the size of an automobile. This brought a new era to Sterling Creek. Newspapers reported that the hydraulics were stripping the overburden at the rate of 800 cubic yards per day. The first cleanup produced $27,987 in gold at an operating expense of $7,408. Sterling Creek gold had a high silver content, giving it a distinctive pale color. The nuggets were coarse and appeared to have been pounded, as most of them were large and thin. One nugget was the size of a man's hand but so thin it weighed only two ounces.

To gain possession of the Sterling Mine, Captain A. P. Ankeny traded a full city block in the heart of Portland on which stood the New Market Theater, the most lavish in the Pacific Northwest. Newspaper stories told of a beautiful display of gold from the Sterling Mine, valued at $10,000.

During the early days Chinese were not

Early water powered arrastra near Jacksonville, used to grind the quartz and separate the gold.

David P. Thompson took control of the Sterling placer mine near Jacksonville, Oregon on June 7, 1877 and by 1878 he completed the building of 23 miles of ditch carrying an ample supply of water to the mine. Two hydraulics were installed with pressure enough to move boulders the size of an automobile. In 1879, he traded the mine to A. P. Ankeny for the New Market Theater in Portland. Thompson, as a boy of 19, walked every step of the way from Ohio driving a herd of cattle. He became Territorial Governor of Idaho, served in the Oregon Legislature and served two terms as mayor of Portland.

The New Market Theater was Portland's first venture into the theatrical arts, built in 1875 by Alexander P. Ankeny, a man who found success in several mining enterprises. It has been described as a scene of dazzling brilliance under the glamour of hundreds of gas jets. At a time when Portland's population was only 12,000, the Pacific Northwest's finest had a seating capacity of 1,200. Box seats sold for from $4 to $75; the dress circle, $1.00 and reserved seats were 25 cents extra; gallery seats sold for fifty cents. Artists came from everywhere to perform on the stage in Portland. The building still stands and is located between First and Second and between S.W. Oak and Ankeny Streets. In 1879, Mr. Ankeny traded the theater and the entire city block to David P. Thompson for the Sterling placer mine near Jacksonville in southern Oregon.

Courtesy Oregon Historical Society

A Chinese gang boss who came to Southern Oregon during the hunt for gold.

The wife of a wealthy Chinese mine owner. In later years Orientals were allowed to own mines and thus were quite successful working over ground abandoned by the white miners.

Gin Lin came to southern Oregon as a gang boss over Chinese working in the mines. Later he was allowed to own his own property and he became wealthy. Later he retired to his native land only to be murdered on the dock.

allowed to own mining property, but hundreds of them worked under Chinese bosses, their wages as little as twenty-five cents a day. Later the white miners relaxed the restriction, and the Chinese began to mine on their own. It wasn't long until Gin Lin, a former Chinese boss, owned several mines. When he finally sold his American interests, he was a rich man. He sailed home to his native land, only to be murdered and robbed on the docks almost as soon as he left the ship.

As a rule white miners were cruel to Chinese and Indians, and quick to take advantage of them. Killing an Oriental was hardly considered a crime. Once a drunken miner shot and killed a Chinese on the streets of Jacksonville without cause. He was brought to trial and fined for shooting a gun within the city limits.

"All you had to do was shout 'gold' and ere the echo could come back from the neighboring hills, there would be before your eyes several hundred assorted prospectors, a saloon fully equipped, and a burying preacher," wrote Erick Bromberg in the *Oregon Historical Quarterly*.

There were two boomtowns on Sterling Creek — Sterlingville at the Sterling Mine, with a reported population of 1,500, and Buncom at the mouth of Sterling Creek.[29] Today there is no more evidence of the towns than of the gold that made them. Nature has healed all but the ugly scars left by the placer mine. Rich placer ground was worked at Kerbyville, now known as Kerby, on the Illinois River.* There was Phoenix on Bear Creek, Allentown near Takelma, Beavertown on Althouse Creek, Sucker Creek, Briggs, Galice, Graves, Foots, Sardine, Forest, Powell, Palmer, and Golden on Coyote Creek. All had their cry of "gold," their moment of glory. The estimated take from Forest Creek was more than $1,000,000.

Prospectors discovered gold in the beach sands, such as at Gold Beach, Pistol River, Ophir, Port Orford, Cape Blanco, and Bandon. One of the early-day gold strikes was made on the beaches north of the Coquille River, and two trappers found gold in Coquille Valley at a place called Whiskey Run.

*Today you will find an interesting little museum at Kerby.

Gold scales used by the Chinese in the early days.

A Chinese yoke used for carrying heavy objects.

One of many wives of wealthy Gin Lin, southern Oregon Chinese mine owner. Each year he would sell or trade his old model to a friend, then back to China for a new one.

Chinese could not own mines in the early days but they worked in them for as little as 25¢ a day; patience they had, as shown by this man quietly fishing.

The old channel gravel deposits just west of Galice, Oregon on a bench about 500 feet above the present stream beds. The picture shows the first high ditch under construction in 1860. Most of the placer gold taken from Galice placers probably came from the old channel deposit.

Courtesy Oregon Historical Society

Courtesy Oregon Historical Society

Jack Sutten photograph

The old general store at Galice in southern Oregon. Gold was discovered here in 1852 by Dr. Louis Galice.

The use of the sluice box was one of the earliest and cheapest methods of washing gravel. By use of pick and shovel, gold bearing gravel is shoveled into a stream of water in a flume with slats in the bottom; gold being heavy sinks to the bottom and is caught above the slats while the gravel is washed away.

Early-day prospector panning for gold in Josephine County.

They sold their claim to a new owner who cleaned up $80,000 from the 20-by-20-foot strip.[30]

Southern Oregon was famous for a class of prospectors known as pocket hunters. These pockets were rich concentrations of lode gold, usually near the surface. Jackson and Josephine counties were considered pocket country. The Johnson and Bowden pockets, known as the Town Mine near Jacksonville, yielded $90,000.[31] The Roaring Gimlet pocket at the mouth of China Gulch yielded $40,000,[32] while the Briggs pocket at the head of Thompson Creek in Josephine County produced $32,000 in two weeks from a narrow cut ten feet long and seven feet deep. Another $18,000 was taken from the pocket before it was cleaned out.[33]

The Jewett Mine, two and a half miles southeast of Grants Pass, yielded $40,000 — almost on the surface. The Gold Hill pocket mine, discovered in 1857, was the granddaddy of them all, producing $700,000. The

Courtesy Oregon Historical Society

The rich Gold Hill pocket mine is located in Jackson County, Sec. 14, T36S.R3W. It was the granddaddy of all pocket mines. It was discovered in 1857 and at least $700,000 was taken from this small surface pocket.

David Briggs holding chunk of nearly pure gold from the "Briggs Pocket Mine" at the head of Thompson Creek in Josephine County. This pocket produced $32,000 in two weeks from a narrow cut ten feet long and seven feet deep. Later another $18,000 was taken from the same pocket before it was cleaned out.

Courtesy Grants Pass Courier

Murphy-Murray dredge on Foots Creek, Jackson County. Capacity 4,000 cubic yards daily, electric powered, 67 buckets of 3½ foot capacity; dug 20 feet below water line.

Courtesy Oregon State Dept. Geology & Mineral Industries

From 1898 to 1902, new modern methods caused a boom in underground mining. The pneumatic or mechanized drilling took the place of hand drilling, doubling production.

View at the Greenback Mine on Tom East Creek, showing 40-stamp mill; discovered in 1897, first worked with an arrastra; 7,000 ft. of tunnels on 12 levels. Estimated production $3,500,000.

Revenue pocket, five miles south of Gold Hill, produced $100,000.[34] The Steamboat pocket on Brush Creek, two miles west of Steamboat, reportedly produced $350,000.[35]

At least three-fourths of the gold in southwestern Oregon produced after 1850 came from placer mining or surface diggings, known as "poor man's mining." During surface mining many fine underground veins were uncovered. But the early-day miner didn't have the machinery, equipment, or know-how to go underground, called lode mining. At a later date, when lode mining did develop in southwestern Oregon, the bulk of the gold came from six mines. Of this group, only the Greenback and the Ashland produced more than $1,000,000.[36] The output from the other four — the Sylanite, Oregon Bull, Lucky Bart, and Opp in Jackson County — ran from $500,000 to $1,000,000. There were at least fourteen other lode mines that produced $100,000 or more.[37]

"This type of mining in southern Oregon

has great possibilities and to this date has barely scratched the surface," declared *Gold and Silver in Oregon*, published by the Oregon State Department of Geology and Mineral Industries in 1968. But the early-day placer-type of mining in the area is perhaps dead — first, because the virgin gold found on the surface has been mined out to a large degree and second, because water once used for hydraulic mining has in late years been directed to irrigation.

Many good lode mines exist in southern Oregon which could be producing today if the price of gold had not been set and held at thirty-five dollars a troy ounce while the cost of labor and materials continued to climb to a point where it was no longer profitable to mine. The War Production Board's Administrative Order L-208 in 1942 during World War II was designed to stop gold mining and force miners to seek employment in base-metal mines such as copper. It was not successful in its purpose, but gold mining has never recovered from this blow.

Regardless of the future, gold mining was

Horse powered arrastra used in southern Oregon

No. 1 — Miles of tunnels were dug in the hills of southern Oregon during the period of hard rock mining.

No. 2 — The same mine as No. 1 years later after mine was abandoned.

once the mainstay of the economy and growth of the state. Gold mining opened the state for settlement by helping to control the Indians and by producing a market for its incoming settlers. It built roads and schools, developed transportation and communication, and promoted law and order.

Placer mining in southwestern Oregon produced millions of dollars during the early years in our history when gold was sorely needed to bolster the nation's economy. It has been estimated that the amount was in the neighborhood of $31,000,000 during the first ten years.[37] Several years of research by the writer have not substantiated any actual amount for this period; our government didn't keep records of gold sources until 1880. The U.S. Mint was located in San Francisco. Gold arrived by pack train, by boat, by overland stage, and by hundreds of miners returning south from the northern diggings. Much, but not all of it, reached the mint. Chinese returning south carried their own gold, much of it no doubt finding its way to the Orient.

There is no evidence of design or plan to shortchange Oregon and the Pacific Northwest in production figures, but there is little doubt that we were shortchanged. There was confusion over the boundary line between Oregon and California, and it is interesting to note that California's yearly production figures just about doubled when gold was discovered in Oregon.[38]

While an effort should be made to set the record straight, we must not lose track of the impact the discovery of gold in California had upon our state. Oregon can thank California for helping her develop her natural resources. Millions of dollars worth of produce were shipped to the mines in the south; shiploads of lumber arrived in San Francisco and Sacramento from Oregon. In 1850 there were 24,000 head of cattle in Oregon west of the Cascades, raised on 1,164 farms; by 1860 the total had soared to 154,131 head, with thousands being ship-

Hauling hydraulic pipe mule back to the placer mines in southern Oregon, before there were roads.

Small placers like the Mountain Slide Mine in southern Oregon were in operation over most of the area where there was water.

ped south to the mines. The first apples sent to California sold for one to five dollars each; most were raised by Oregon's pioneer nurserymen, Luelling and Meek at Milwaukie. The first shipment of 200 pounds of apples to San Francisco in 1853 sold for $500; and in 1854, forty bushels brought $2,500. Even in Portland in 1856, three boxes of Winesap apples sold for $102.[39] These were the first signs that southern Oregon was changing from mining to farming.

Oregon became a state on February 14, 1859. Communication was so slow it was a month before people in Oregon received word. The news traveled by telegraph to St. Louis, from there by Butterfield Overland

Stage to San Francisco, and by the steamer *Brother Jonathan* to Portland, arriving early in the morning on March 5. On that date only 2,874 people lived in Portland.

During an eleven-year period from 1849 until 1860, the year after statehood and just at the start of the Civil War, Oregon's population west of the Cascade Mountains jumped from 9,083 to 52,465. Western Oregon was growing.[40]

In the vast land east of the Cascades, however, there were only 1,689 newcomers by 1860, and most of them lived close to the military post at The Dalles. The entire area was known as Wasco County.

This was ten years after the discovery of gold in southern Oregon. Men everywhere were restless, for the Civil War was just beginning. Many of them returned from the goldfields to their Willamette Valley farms, while others drifted north still looking for the golden rainbow. There was a great demand for gold reserves for our international credit; the U.S. Treasury was empty.

The government resorted to issuing notes with little or no gold to back them up. They were accepted everywhere in the East where there was no gold, but the gold-producing states on the Pacific Coast refused to take them at face value, calling them "Lincoln Skins." A dollar bill was worth seventy-nine cents. Later, when the outcome of the Civil War was in doubt, the value dropped to as low as thirty-seven cents.[41]

In mining towns like Canyon City, paper money was not accepted by stores, saloons, and other business houses except at a large discount. William Kane at Canyon City killed his employer because he paid him in paper money. It's a bit gruesome, but Kane's skull may be seen at the Grant County Museum in Canyon City. It was risky to use Lincoln Skins in some parts of the Old West!

Placer mining on Wolf Creek in southern Oregon

Hauling ore from the mines near Takalma, in front of the Golden Rule store in Grants Pass.

STUMP TOWN TALE OF GOLD

ON A WARM SUMMER DAY IN JULY 1861, a group of men was clustered on Front Street in Portland, listening intently to a story about a lost gold mine. The speaker was I. L. Adams, who claimed he'd been a member of the lost wagon train of 1845. He told them about some gold nuggets picked up along a stream in eastern Oregon and said he had since been back to the site, only to be driven away by Indians. He volunteered with some generosity to lead a party to the mine, provided a strong enough group could be organized.

This event was later to change the destiny of Portland. The community had been growing, steadily but slowly. It had managed to throw off the nickname of "Stump Town" and was becoming a solid metropolis as the center of commerce and coastal trade.

There is some confusion about the exact birthdate of Portland. We do know that in 1842 William Johnson built a log cabin for his Indian wife and children near what is now Southwest Macadam Avenue and Curry Street. In 1843 A. L. Lovejoy and William Overton arrived at the site known as The Clearing and that winter acquired a land claim covering what is now downtown Portland. Overton worked for Lovejoy and took half the land in payment for services. In 1844 he sold his part to Francis W. Pettygrove for $50. Lovejoy and Pettygrove were now partners; Lovejoy had received his half of downtown Portland for a filing fee of twenty-five cents, while Pettygrove had to pay $50.

In 1845 the two partners platted sixteen blocks of the townsite. Lovejoy wanted to name the new town Boston, while Pettygrove preferred Portland. They settled the argument by the flip of a coin, and Pettygrove won.

Daniel H. Lownsdale established a tannery about where the Multnomah Club is today and in 1848 purchased the entire Portland townsite for $5,000 worth of tanned leather. The sale included a wharf at the foot of Washington Street.

Captain John Couch, a seafaring man in the Columbia River trade, was the first to recognize the importance of Portland's strategic location, and he made the town his headquarters. At this early date East Portland was a forest of trees with little cross-river traffic; the first ferryboat was a canoe.

Pettygrove opened the first store at Front and Washington Streets in 1845. Job McNemee had the first log hotel, known as the Ohio House, where weary people could spread their blankets. He also operated a butcher shop. James Terwilliger built a blacksmith shop in 1846. McNemee and Terwilliger were both members of the lost wagon train of 1845.

In 1847 Captain Nathaniel Crosby, great-grandfather of entertainer Bing Crosby, erected the first frame house in Portland on the southwest corner of First and Washington Streets. Crosby shipped the lumber twenty thousand miles around Cape Horn.

About 800 people lived in Portland when this picture of Front Street was taken in 1852. Ten years later, when the gold stampede east of the Cascades got under way, the population was around 2,900. Yet during the opening three year period of the gold rush, it is estimated that 82,000 people passed through Portland enroute to the gold fields in eastern Oregon and Idaho.

Starting in 1847 a number of emigrants were attracted to the new town and built homes there. The First Methodist Church was erected in 1848. Colonel William King built the first water-powered sawmill in 1849, at the time when the mother lode was being overrun with prospectors and Portland was almost deserted by able-bodied men. The following year Adams and Reed completed the first steam sawmill. Indian villages stood on the edge of town; when the sawmill opened the steam whistle for celebration, the Indians were so frightened they vanished like quail on the opening day of hunting season.

A log cabin post office was established in 1849 on the corner of Southwest Front Avenue and Washington Street, with Thomas Smith as postmaster. In 1850, the year California gained statehood, *The Orego-nian* began weekly publication under the direction of T. J. Dryer.

Stump Town was growing up, with a population around eight hundred.

Hugh D. O'Bryant became the first mayor in 1851, in an election where 222 people cast their votes. At the time Portland was incorporated it was part of Washington County, so citizens from Portland had to travel to Hillsboro to hold court. Multnomah County was created in 1854 from Washington and Clackamas counties. In that same year, Thomas Fraser founded the first public school.

In 1855 the first ferryboat was placed in service across the Willamette River. The land on the east bank was leveled of timber to what is now Grand Avenue. Portland's timber had long since been cleared, although the stumps remained, painted white

Courtesy Oregon Historical Society

This is the first frame house ever built in Portland. It was located on the southwest corner of First and Washington Streets. Later, as you can see, it was used for business. It was built by Captain Nathaniel Crosby, great-grandfather of Bing Crosby, in 1847. The first couple ever married in Portland and the ceremony took place here.

Courtesy Oregon Historical Society

The weekly *Oregonian* was established on December 4, 1850. On this date Portland had a sawmill, a log hotel known as the Ohio House, and Front Street from Burnside to Jefferson was cleared of timber, but the stumps were painted white so that people could avoid them at night.

Portland in 1878 looking east; when a ferryboat was the only connection between the east and west sides of the river. At that time, the east side was not even a part of Portland.

During the 1880s and the late 1890s, Portland harbor became a no-man's land for sailors and country boys looking for adventure at sea, and captains of departing ships were always short handed. Many an unsuspecting young man was fed doctored whiskey, dope or just plain black-jacked on the dark streets, robbed of his money and placed on board a departing ship. The usual fee the captain paid was from $50 to $150 per man.

In the 1870s, a golden harvest of wheat started to pour down the Columbia River by boat from the new wheat fields in eastern Oregon. Each fall, 90 sailing vessels entered Portland harbor carrying produce to all parts of the world. By 1874, wheat exports came to $11,105,850, the bulk to the United Kingdom. From 1873 to 1879, Oregon exported 28,300,000 pounds of wool, most of it came from eastern Oregon. In 1870, 25,000 boxes of apples were shipped to the United Kingdom. By 1875, Oregon exported 231,500 cases of salmon. By 1880, Portland was well established as a harbor and terminus for 57 shipping lines.

for nighttime visibility. The ferry linked the two towns and other budding villages along the riverbank. James B. Stephens had purchased the site of East Portland in 1845 and five years later laid out the town, which grew in time, especially after the coming of the Oregon-California railroad along the east bank. In 1891 East Portland and Albina became officially a part of the west bank metropolis, although for years, East Portland maintained its own railroad station.

Until the Willamette was spanned by the first Morrison Bridge, opened in April 1887, the ferry linked the twin cities and proved a busy, profitable enterprise. Charges were all the traffic would bear:

Foot passengers .... 10 cents
Man and horse .... 25 cents
Wagon and team .... 62.5 cents
Each additional animal .... 10 cents
Cart or buggy with one animal .... 50 cents
Horses, mules, cattle, per head .... 10 cents
Sheep, hogs (each) .... 5 cents
100 pounds freight not in wagon .... 10 cents

Powerful men of the community owned the ferry and, knowing that a bridge would put the ferry out of business, used political influence to delay construction for many years. The owners were right: the bridge was opened and the ferry was terminated. When one thinks of the network of bridges spanning the river today, and the ever-increasing traffic, it's difficult to believe that this was little more than eighty years ago — within the memory of people still living.

For years Oregon City, then known as Willamette Falls, was considered the logical place for a big city, while Portland was not highly regarded. In 1842 Willamette Falls was a sizable community, and in that year a plat was made and the town became known as Oregon City. Meanwhile, Portland had only a single log cabin. But by 1850, the downriver town's population reached 800, while Oregon City had only 889; Portland was marching ahead, with a more convenient location and a better harbor.

Captain John C. Ainsworth, who arrived in 1850, was among the most prominent of Oregon's pioneer citizens. His faith was in Portland, and he made the Willamette and Columbia rivers work for Oregon. Noticing that all Oregon's imports and exports moved by boat, Ainsworth became the leading spirit in the founding of the Oregon Steam Navigation Company, which controlled all parts of the Columbia and Willamette rivers for many years. The gold rush to California and later to southern Oregon established Portland as Oregon's principal seaport and shipping center.

Many people moved in and out of Portland, for business and pleasure. The New York was the leading hotel, known from San Francisco to Port Angeles and from Portland to St. Louis as the "two-bit house," a place where men flopped for the night between coastal steamers and riverboats. The Franklin House, a place of more refinement, charged fifty cents, while meals cost seventy-five cents. The Farmer House rates

Oregon became a state on February 14, 1859, yet the communication between east and west was so slow it was not known in the state until March 5. The news came by telegraph to St. Louis, and from St. Louis to San Francisco by Butterfield Overland State, and by the steamer, Brother Jonathan, to Portland arriving at 4:00 A.M. This picture shows the celebration held on Front Street. On that date, there were only 2,874 people living here.

were: lodging per night, 25 cents; board by the week with three meals per day, $5.00; single meals, 25 cents.

Travel was on the increase. Portlanders could travel south by land or sea. All mail arrived by Overland Stage from St. Louis to San Francisco and then by ship to Portland. No other means of communication existed with the East — no telegraph, no telephone. Oregon was connected with the outside world, but the contact was tedious and slow.[42]

That was how conditions stood on a certain July day of 1861 when I. L. Adams spoke of gold on Front Street. Among listeners were four men who had drifted north from the goldfields of California. They were Henry Griffin, David Littlefield, William Stafford and F. W. Schriver. The four agreed to arrange a prospecting party, and in August fifty men, led by Adams, began the long journey into eastern Oregon. Each had a

Oregon became a state on February 14, 1859. It was the steamship, Brother Jonathan, that carried the news to Portland arriving on the morning of March 5. During the gold rush this ship carried $1,357,835 in gold dust from Portland to San Francisco from September 24, 1863 to November 5, 1864. On July 1865 the Brother Jonathan was lost at sea. One hundred sixty-six persons aboard were drowned, only 19 saved. The ship's safe contained $200,000 in gold coins and a million dollars in gold bullion.

saddle horse, a pack horse, a rifle, and plenty of ammunition.

After a period of time it became apparent that I. L. Adams had never been over the route. To save his life, he signed a paper stating he had lied and that he wasn't a member of the lost wagon train. He was turned loose, without horse or gun, to find his way back to the Willamette Valley alone. Most of the men returned to their homes. The rest of the party, including the four men from California and a few from the mines in southern Oregon, headed northeast toward the Burnt River, expecting to move west over the Oregon Trail. The group prospected as they traveled. On October 23, 1861, Henry Griffin dug a hole down to bedrock where he struck pay dirt that ran from fifty cents to $1.50 a pan. The location is now known as Griffin Gulch, a tributary of the Powder River, only a few miles from the city of Baker.[43]

While this group was unable to locate the Lost Blue Bucket Mine, they did find gold in eastern Oregon. Little did they realize that this strike and others to follow would lead to a stampede. It has been estimated that in little more than a year thirty thousand men were engaged in mining.[44]

Twenty-two men were in the discovery

Courtesy Oregon Historical Society

This is the gravestone of H. H. Griffin, the man who discovered gold in eastern Oregon. There is no picture of the man who started the gold rush, even his name is spelled wrong.

party. All but four staked their claims and then headed for home to spend the winter. Griffin, Littlefield, Stafford, and Schriver remained — the first white men to spend a winter in the area. They hurriedly built a small cabin before the snow arrived.

The winter of 1861-62 was among the coldest in history, with snow reaching a depth of fourteen feet. When spring came the horses were skin and bones, having survived on sagebrush and willow bark. Supplies were desperately low, so Littlefield and Schriver headed over the mountains with one horse to Fort Walla Walla. They paid for their supplies from a poke of gold, which caused no little excitement.

Orlando Humason, a gold buyer from The Dalles, was at the fort returning from newly discovered mines in Idaho. Since this was the first gold from eastern Oregon, Humason purchased it. With an idea for more business, he placed the yellow nuggets in a showcase in Portland.

The cry of a new gold strike in Oregon spread like a grass fire, and within days the four discoverers were surrounded by miners.

David Littlefield, a member of the party which discovered gold in Griffin Gulch on October 21, 1861. He traded a poke full of gold for supplies at Fort Walla Walla. It was this gold that started the gold rush that helped to settle all of Oregon east of The Dalles.

AUBURN WAS OUT AHEAD

AUBURN WAS ONCE THE LARGEST TOWN in Oregon; today you can hardly find the townsite, a few miles southwest of Baker. Yet it was the first Oregon center east of The Dalles.

Auburn came into being in 1862, during a roaring gold strike when 1,700 mining claims were filed between May and August. William Packwood called a meeting in June and is listed as one of the founders — along with Ed Cranston and George Hall. In six months there was a population of 5,000 on one street about a mile long, from Freezeout Gulch to Blue Canyon. Seven hundred cabins were raised within a year and again as many tents, plus three general stores, two hotels, several boardinghouses, three saloons and gambling houses, three butcher shops, two blacksmith shops, three livery stables, a school, a portable sawmill, a stout jail, and a Masonic Hall. The preacher was slow to arrive, so there was no church. Now and then a circuit rider preached in the street on Sunday.

Auburn became the first seat of Baker County in June 1862. The post office was established the following November. There were 151 families then, with 314 children. The bulk of the population was male, nearly all white with the exception of a few Chinese. As with all early mining camps, there were women following a trade older than the hills.

Pack trains supplied the miners with the necessities of life, over a route 300 miles long. Flour sold for $28 a hundred; bacon,

50 cents a pound; eggs, 25 cents each; sugar, 45 cents a pound. Whiskey arrived in five-gallon wooden barrels, two to a mule. The saloonkeeper served a watered-down mixture fortified with plug tobacco shavings — it's no wonder the town was a brawling place. Merchants charged double the cost, and there was never a shortage of whiskey or someone to consume it.

Two outlaws were placed in the Auburn hoosegow for robbery. They asked for pen and paper. Within a short time they handed the sheriff the following note:

"On the trail we met two fools,
and took from them their horses and mules,
we left with them their pocket knives,
which served perhaps to save their lives."

The sheriff wrote in reply:

"When bad boys steal horses and mules
Auburn lets them hang around for a while."

They did, until someone cut them down.

Spanish Tom was hanged for killing two men in a card game. French Pete was hanged for placing strychnine in his partner's flour. The town was as wild and untamed as the vast countryside around it.

Many emigrants on their way to the Willamette Valley were caught up by the gold rush and stayed to become pioneer Baker County residents. Finding Auburn crowded, some moved on to other fields — Boise Basin, the Owyhee mines, Mormon Basin, Rye Valley, Sumpter, and Granite. Wherever there was a mountain stream,

Courtesy Oregon Historical Society

William H. Packwood was in the army when he first came to Oregon. He was a friend of Lincoln and a signer of the Oregon Constitution. He was only 30 years old when gold was discovered in eastern Oregon. He helped found Auburn, the first town east of The Dalles. Packwood became Baker County's first school superintendent; he married the first school teacher in the county. He was a pioneer stockman, storekeeper, miner, toll road and ferry boat operator, hotel keeper and above all, Oregon's greatest ditch digger during the mining days. He promoted the Auburn, Sanger, Sparta and Eldorado Ditches. The Eldorado was the grand-daddy of all ditches, 130 miles long. His grandson is now United States Senator for Oregon.

A McCord photograph

George Washington Hall became Baker County's first sheriff in June 1862. He helped lay out Auburn, the first town east of The Dalles. Later Hall operated a hotel in Bourne.

It's a pity, but this is the only authentic picture of Auburn in Baker County where gold was discovered in Oregon. Within one year there were 700 homes, as many tents, stores, saloons, hotels and 5,000 people; for a while the largest town in Oregon.

Courtesy Oregon Historical Society

The writer with foot on stump of the old hangman's tree at Auburn where gold was first discovered in Oregon. Spanish Tom killed two men in a card game, he was hung from this tree. French Pete was hung from the same tree for putting strychnine in his partner's flour.

men could be found digging for gold. Some were lucky, others were not. Some turned to farming and a life much more satisfying than prospecting for gold.

Auburn was destined to live but a short while. When the easy pickings were gone, so were the white miners. The Chinese inherited Auburn more or less by default, and for a number of years one could hear their chatter in the evenings as they engaged in their one great obsession — gambling.

Today Auburn has the distinction of being the town where gold was discovered in eastern Oregon — and little else. Before it became a complete ghost town, the county seat was moved to Baker City.

Henry Griffin, the man who made the discovery, rests in his grave just a short way from where his shovel revealed the hidden treasure. Few people today have ever heard of Auburn, and few realize that a poke of nuggets started a gold rush that helped to settle all of eastern Oregon. No actual record exists of the amount of gold taken. Two Frenchmen on Blue Gulch panned out $100,000, and 1,700 mining claims were recorded in the district that used water from the Auburn ditch, so the take should have been rather high. The Sumpter newspaper, *Blue Mountain American,* stated in 1902 that Auburn placers produced an estimated $10,000,000. It is strange that no worthwhile pictures endure of this colorful old town which was once the key to eastern Oregon.[45]

Chinese shovel found in eastern Oregon's gold fields. Chinese lettering on handle.

Home made pick, gold mould for making gold bricks, and a mercury flask all found at Auburn.

OUTFITTERS FOR THE MINES

LONG BEFORE THE INDIANS had any knowledge of the white man, the present location of The Dalles was known as "Win-quatt," meaning a place encircled by high rocks or cliffs. It was at Win-quatt that Lewis and Clark stopped to rest on their long journey overland to the Pacific Ocean. It was also known as "Wasco-Pum," and the first post office was under that name. The French voyageurs with the Hudson's Bay Company called The Dalles rapids "La Dalle," meaning the swift trough of the Columbia River.

When the great westward migration started to move along the Oregon Trail in 1842, The Dalles was called "The Landing." It was the end of the 2,000-mile overland trip and the start of the treacherous journey on rafts down the Columbia River to the Willamette. Not until 1846 and 1847 was the Barlow toll road completed around Mt. Hood to bypass the river—although the road was considered almost as treacherous.

In 1850 the regular army established a post at Fort Dalles. The Territorial Legislature then created Wasco County — a massive area comprised of what is now eastern Oregon, all of Idaho, parts of Wyoming and Washington. Dalles City was named county seat, and the courthouse was the first east of the Cascades. Other than the few people living in the town, only about three hundred settlers occupied the entire county. Nevertheless, in 1857 the town was incorporated. Later the Post Office Department changed the name to The Dalles. Even as late as 1860, one year before the discovery of gold east of the Cascade Mountains, there were only sixteen hundred people in all of Wasco County, including The Dalles.

During the first three years of the eastern Oregon gold rush, steamship records alone show that more than 82,000 people moved up the Columbia River into this vast country. The Dalles, on the edge of the frontier, became the jumping-off place for the wilderness, the last outfitting point. Miners, prospectors, opportunists, dreamers — all came through The Dalles. Most traveled up the Columbia by boat. Others used their old prairie schooners, rode horseback leading a packhorse or mule, or came on foot. The Dalles was truly the gateway to the mines."

Almost overnight the permanent population jumped from 250 to 2,500. Fred Lockley, in his book *History of the Columbia River Valley* says as many as 10,000 people were in The Dalles at one time waiting for passage upriver or for the 200-mile trail trip to the mines at Canyon City. For a few days at a time The Dalles was three times larger than Portland.

Each prospector heading into the hills needed to outfit himself with pick, shovel, gold pan, axe, magnifying glass, cooking pots, clothing, blankets, tent, tarp, gun and ammunition, rubber boots, bacon, beans, coffee, and flour. Most included tobacco and whiskey. Added to this was a good mule or horse, priced at from $150 to $200, plus a complete pack outfit. The wilderness could supply none of these things.

Wasco Courthouse

One of the first log cabins built at Wascopum now know as
The Dalles.

The Farmers Hotel in The Dalles with the hotel bus in
foreground.

Oregon Steam Navigation Co. office at The Dalles, during
the gold rush days of the early 1860s.

The Dalles was the jumping-off place and last outfitting
headquarters for those seeking gold east of the Cascades.
For three years the steamers averaged 200 people a day.
The Dalles, with a population of 2,500, found it nothing
unusual to have 10,000 people waiting there to be outfitted
to go inland to the mines.

The Dalles in 1867 showing Globe Hotel

Bloch-Miller and Company in The Dalles became the largest outfitting store in the state. It was also the largest buyer of gold, averaging $50,000 a month for the first three years. While gold at the mint in San Francisco was priced at $20.70 a troy ounce, Bloch-Miller gave $17.00 an ounce for gold from Canyon City and Florence, Idaho. Gold-carrying silver alloy was priced at $14.00 an ounce, with copper alloy somewhat less. So much gold was flowing to The Dalles that the citizens petitioned Congress to build a mint; $125,000 was appropriated and a building was constructed, but because of politics the mint never went into operation. Later the building was used as a flour mill.

The saloons and merchants accepted gold dust as a medium of exchange. A silver 25-cent piece was the smallest coin in use. Gold coins ran from $1.00 to $5.00, and there were a few $50.00 gold "slugs"

minted at Oregon City. A good cigar sold for 50 cents.

George Clayton ran the largest gambling house in the state, open day and night. There was plenty of action: poker, faro, three-card monte — you name it. The sky was the limit and everyone carried a gun or, as they said, "went well heeled." The only deterrent to crime was not knowing how fast the stranger across the table would be on the draw. There were thirty-six saloons at the height of the gold rush. Then there were such dives as "Irish Moll's Place" and the "Golden Rule" presided over by Madam De Bilk.

The famous Umatilla House, built at the boat landing in 1857, was a mint in itself. More money passed over its bar than any of the others. It was a center of activity for dining, dancing, and drinking. The dining room seated 250 people. Meals were 25 cents and rooms 25 cents. There were 123

Courtesy Oregon Historical Society

Looking down Main Street in The Dalles during the great flood. The building at the extreme right in the distance is the famous Umatilla Hotel.

The Dalles suffered from several early-day floods, but the granddaddy of all floods came in May and June of 1894. The Columbia River reached 59 feet, seven inches above low water. The water was one-and-one half feet deep in the office of the *Times-Mountaineer*. No mail east or west for several days; the only dry place was in the brewery. Salmon were caught in the streets. Frank Seufert lost all his fishwheels.

Courtesy Oregon Historical Society

WELLS, FARGO & CO'S EXPRESS.

Wells, Fargo & Company's express receipt for $1,300 in gold dust being shipped from The Dalles to San Francisco.

The first newspaper in The Dalles was called *The Dalles Journal*, established there in March 1859. Later the name was changed to *The Mountaineer*. The three most widely read newspapers in eastern Oregon during the gold rush were *The Bedrock Democrat* in Baker City, *The Blue Mountain Eagle* in John Day and Canyon City, and *The Mountaineer* in The Dalles. A wealth of information can be found in their files, yellowed with age.

This early picture of The Dalles shows the unfinished United States Mint in the foreground. In the early 1860s, with millions of raw gold coming from the mines in eastern Oregon and Idaho, gold miners and businessmen petitioned Congress to build a mint on the Columbia River. The Dalles was picked as the logical location. In 1865 Congress appropriated $125,000 and construction was started. The plans called for a two-story stone building with a fireplace in each room. The floors were designed to support the heavy coin-making machines. There were many delays. The first superintendent was drowned when the steamer, Brother Jonathan, sank off the coast of California. Then politics entered the picture, and the mint was never completed.

Saloon in The Dalles; gambling room through swinging doors in the back. Piano on right has pipe railing to protect it from customers with too much Panther Juice.

The recreation room in the Umatilla House with its late newspapers and magazines, card room and pool tables was the winter headquarters for many miners with gold in their pockets and fun in their hearts — easy come, easy go. The dining room with its great glass chandeliers was the town's social center. The owners, Nick Sinnott and Dan Handley, had only one rule — No one was ever to be turned away for lack of funds for a meal or a bed.

rooms with a stove in each, two bathrooms, and a toilet in the basement. Also stored in the basement were 2,500 gallons of whiskey.

Vic Trevitt, who became state senator from Wasco County, ran the Mt. Hood Saloon. It was more or less a gentlemen's club — no gambling, no drunks, and no rough talk. His saloon could have been called an island in a sea of sin. At night the narrow streets were aglare with lights from saloons and gambling halls. Mary St. Clair ran a hurdy-gurdy dance hall. She charged the boys $20 for a bottle of champagne, but when their luck changed and they were down and out she was the first to lend a helping hand. Most miners were young, looking for fun as well as gold, and many of them wintered in The Dalles. After a summer of hard work and with a poke full of treasure, it was easy come, easy go.

When inland towns were first established, merchants from Boise, Walla Walla, Missoula, and all of eastern Oregon came to The Dalles to buy supplies. Before the portage between The Dalles and Celilo Falls was completed and before the steamers started operating on the upper river to Umatilla Landing and Lewiston, long lines of freight wagons and mule trains moved from The Dalles to the back country. For many years the colorful river port remained outfitting headquarters for the mines.[46]

The lobby of the Umatilla House with its great brass cuspidors, long mahogany counter, its hotel register and pigeonholes behind the desk with its dozens of keys. The walls were papered with bright red flowers and behind glass was a printed schedule for the arrival and departure of the riverboats. The pungent odor of tobacco permeated the room. The cellar was the bar room, the bar of solid mahogany with huge plate glass mirrors; more money passed over its bar than any other in the state. Two thousand five hundred gallons of whiskey was on hand at all times. When lucky miners returned with a poke full of gold, one could hear the popping of champagne corks at the bar.

The Umatilla House in the early mining days was an imposing structure; three stories in height, painted a light gray, tall windows looking out across the Columbia River, located at the steamboat dock on the water's edge. It was headquarters for traveling miners and merchants both winter and summer, up and down the Columbia River. In this photograph, the river is at flood stage.

DESTINY RIDES THE GOLD BOOM

EVEN WITH HIGH COSTS AND POOR TRANS-PORTATION at the beginning of the eastern Oregon gold rush, thousands of men, horses, mules, and cattle poured up the Columbia River by boat from Portland. Lancaster Pollard, in his book *Oregon and the Pacific Northwest*, writes: "The inland transportation could not have developed by itself. It was the discovery of gold that turned the trick."

The Oregon Steam Navigation Company, known as O.S.N., was owned by such well-known men as John C. Ainsworth, Simeon C. Reed, Robert R. Thompson, William S. Ladd, B. F. Bradford, I. W. Coe, Benjamin Stark, Josiah Myrick, Richard Williams, and George W. Hoyt. Within this group of giants was a mad scramble for control of the lucrative river traffic. In the end the patience of Captain Ainsworth brought this fighting bunch of tomcats to one saucer of cream — namely, the Oregon Steam Navigation Company. They smothered the competition, gained complete control of Columbia River business, and soon owned all the steamboats running from Portland to Lewiston and the mouth of the Clearwater River.

The key to this giant empire lay with the portages. They took control first of the portage at the Cascades, where the town of Cascade Locks is now located, and later the portage above The Dalles and Celilo Falls. The four strong men — Ainsworth, Thompson, Ladd, and Reed — became the dominant figures who ruled the Oregon Steam Navigation Company.

Portland in 1862, with a population of about 3,500, found its hotels, restaurants, saloons, and harbor choked with miners, merchants, farmers, gamblers, dance-hall girls, Chinese, and fortune-seekers of all kinds. Long lines of horse-drawn drays stood for twenty-four hours to get aboard boats heading upriver to the goldfields. Traffic was so heavy that the portage at the Cascades was blocked for days. Steamship records show that 24,500 people traveled upriver from Portland in 1862 and 22,000 the following year. In 1864 the movement grew to 36,000.

Five hundred to two thousand pounds of gold came downstream from the mines twice a week, passing over the portages en route to the mint at San Francisco.

The Cascade portage on the Oregon side of the river was finished in 1856. The detour was six miles long, and the cars were mule-drawn until 1862, with wooden rails covered with iron. When the rush to the mines started, the mules couldn't begin to handle the traffic. The portage was modernized by replacing them with a tiny steam engine called *The Pony*, built in San Francisco and transported north by boat, along with new flatcars. Several small coaches were added, and this became Oregon's first narrow-gauge railroad.

The second portage extended for fifteen miles from The Dalles upriver to Celilo Falls. It was used by people traveling to the mines in Idaho and to the new mining district of Auburn. This was nothing more than

Courtesy Oregon Historical Society

Captain John C. Ainsworth was the man behind the Oregon Steam Navigation Company whose boats carried thousands of men and freight to the gold fields in eastern Oregon and Idaho. Olson, in *Oregon Times and Trails*, said about Ainsworth, "He made the Willamette and Columbia Rivers work for Oregon. The rivers were the arteries that carried the life flood of Oregon and Captain Ainsworth was the pumping heart." Captain Ainsworth died in Oakland, California in 1893.

In order to protect the six-mile portage area at the Cascades on the Columbia, a block house was built on the north side of the river.

Courtesy Oregon Historical Society

Mule Power Train on the Oregon Portage Railroad

a rough wagon road, causing another traffic jam at The Dalles. After this portage was consolidated into the holdings of the O.S.N., the company replaced the wagon road with a second narrow-gauge railroad, at a cost of $50,000 for the fifteen miles.

The O.S.N. owned three groups of boats: one from Portland to the lower Cascade portage, another from the lower Cascade portage to The Dalles, and a third from the upper portage to Umatilla Landing, Wallula, and Lewiston, Idaho. After modernizing the two portages, passengers and freight moved much faster. People heading upriver from Portland had to be on board the steamers early in the morning. They were served breakfast for one dollar and had a choice of ham and eggs, tenderloin steak, loin of venison, fried potatoes, hotcakes, and coffee.

The boats arrived at the Cascade portage just before noon. Passengers and freight were loaded on the portage railroad, and the tiny engine hauled them a distance of six

The portage at the Cascades in 1861 (now known as Cascade Locks) was six miles long. When steamers from Portland unloaded their up-river freight at the Cascades for transport over the portage during the gold rush, the mule-drawn flat cars were so slow that freight sometimes piled up for days before it could be loaded onto steamers above the rapids for transfer to The Dalles.

Peter Britt photograph

People of all nationalities came to the land of gold and golden opportunities. This is a picture of a Holland Dutch family.

The difficulties of the wagon road portage above The Dalles and past Celilo Falls were lessened by the construction in 1863 of the 15-mile narrow gauge Portage Railroad. Built on the Oregon side of the Columbia River at a reported cost of $50,000 per mile and in service until the 1880s, this railroad constituted an important link between the riverboats plying the Columbia between Cascade Locks and The Dalles and those plying the up-river run from Ceilio to Umatilla Landing and Lewiston.

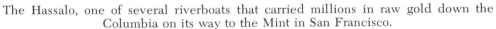

The Hassalo, one of several riverboats that carried millions in raw gold down the Columbia on its way to the Mint in San Francisco.

The dining room on one of the riverboats. The dining room tables were resplendent with silverplate and linen from New York City. A steamboat breakfast consisted of your choice of ham and eggs, tenderloin steak, loin venison, fried potatoes, hotcakes and coffee.

The river steamer, Tenino, on the upper Columbia. With stops at Umatilla Landing, Wallula and Lewiston, this vessel is credited with having taken in $18,000 on one up-river trip in 1863.

miles. Once again freight and passengers were reloaded on the midriver boats. Dinner was served in the dining room with the finest of silver and chinaware. Steamers arrived at The Dalles just before dark.

Most passengers were obliged to stay overnight, many stopping at the Umatilla House. Those bound for the mines at Canyon City remained in town several days to purchase their outfits. For the first two years there was no road; only a rough trail covered the two hundred miles to the mines.

Passengers heading on up the river had to be awake early to ride the portage railroad

The site of old Fort Walla Walla, now known as Wallula

to Celilo. There they boarded the upper-river steamers, arriving at Umatilla Landing in the afternoon. Passengers heading for Fort Walla Walla could expect another overnight stop before continuing to Wallula, where they disembarked. On the following morning the boats moved out to Lewiston, gateway to the mines in Idaho.

Freight and passenger rates were extremely high during the first four years. At the outset of the gold rush, the freight rate from Portland to The Dalles ran from $40 to $50 per ton; the portage charge was $15 a ton. The passenger rate from Portland to The Dalles was $20, and all meals were $1.00. From Portland to Lewiston it was $120 per ton plus portages charges. The passenger fare to Lewiston was $60, plus $1.00 for each meal.[47]

The freight rate averaged one dollar for a single shovel to Lewiston and one dollar for a dozen brooms to Hood River. Rates were ten times higher than any in the entire United States. The company figured forty cubic feet per ton. In measuring a wagon they adopted this method:

1. Measure the wagon at its widest place.
2. Measure the wagon from the tip of the tongue to the back wheels.
3. Lift the tongue up in a vertical position and measure the height from the top of the tongue to the deck.
4. Multiply all together and you get the cubic measurement. Every forty feet is a ton — nothing is deducted for vacuum.

Using this system, a vessel with a 150 net ton register brought in cash almost double the register.

A steer valued at $15 in the Willamette Valley sold for $30 upriver. During the first eight months of 1862, 46,000 head of cattle were transported to the country east of The Dalles. The same is true for horses, mules, sheep, and hogs. The charge on cattle, horses, and mules was $8.00 per head — $1.00 for each sheep and hog.

In 1869 J. Palmer and A. P. Ankeny opened a trail for pack trains and cattle through the Columbia River gorge to The Dalles. Only then did the steamers reduce their rates.

During 1862 the sternwheelers earned 148 per cent on the money invested. Old steamship records at The Dalles show that in April and May $55,736 was received from passenger tickets alone, not considering freight from Celilo portage and the steamers above Celilo Falls. On this same upper-river run the steamer *Tenino* earned $18,000 on one trip and the steamer *Okanagan* paid for itself on her maiden voyage, according to P. W. Gillette writing in 1904 in the *Oregon Historical Quarterly*.

From 1861 to 1864 the O.S.N. transported 60,320 tons of freight, over a third of it in 1864 — 22,000 tons. The boats from Portland to The Dalles averaged two hundred passengers per upriver trip the first few years.[47] Miners returning from the goldfields were charged two ounces of gold dust for the privilege of sleeping on the deck. By 1865 the company operated twenty-nine ships on all sections of the river. Many of them were floating palaces — expensive carpets, beautiful cut-glass chandeliers, elegant hardwood fixtures, and fancy bars with glittering mirrors. Nearly all the furnishings had been shipped around the horn. The O.S.N. also operated thirteen schooners and four barges on the river, about half of them below the Cascade rapids.

A great majority of those traveling upriver were not Oregonians; many came from California and the other states of the union. People from all parts of the globe poured into the new land. To get some idea of the impact of 82,500 newcomers into the area, we must remember that in 1860 there were fewer than 53,000 in the whole state, and most of them lived west of the Cascades. Oregon's population increased thirteen times from 1850 to 1860.

Not all newcomers were miners; the Homestead Act in 1862 gave people the right to file on 160 acres for a fee of $10.

The Dalles City, her upper deck crowded with passengers, is loading horses and sacks of wool; one of several stops the boats made on their trips up and down the Columbia River.

Many of the Oregon Steam Navigation Company's riverboats were equipped with elegant furnishings; Brussels carpets in the cabin and stateroom floors, glittering chandeliers lighted the boats from stem to stern. The picture shows the ornate ladies' room on one of the riverboats. The bars were of hand-carved Mahogany, and were busy all day long.

Thousands of settlers followed the miners into the new land, knowing the prospectors would be a ready market for the crops they raised.

No produce of any kind had ever been grown in all this fertile country. The sharp-eyed farmer realized that thousands of horses and mules were used in the mines and for freighting and packing. Knowing the miner would need meat, and hay and grain for his horses and mules, the homesteader followed in the wake of the gold-seeker,

driving his livestock with him, assured of a captive market. Merchants opened stores, and around the stores mining towns sprang to life.

Umatilla Landing was founded in 1863, after the narrow-gauge railroad was built between The Dalles and Celilo Falls. With boats running on the upper river, the landing grew into an important stop, shortening the distance to 150 miles for wagons and pack trains on their way to Auburn. It was a raw town, open all night and full of tough

Umatilla Landing on the Columbia River. When the upper portage railroad was completed between The Dalles and Celilo Falls in 1863, the landing became the chief shipping point to all the mines around Auburn and the Powder and Burnt River areas and as far east as Boise, Idaho. Within six months there were 100 substantial buildings.

muleskinners and wild-eyed gents with gold in their pockets and a hankering for whiskey. Within six months there were a hundred buildings, including twenty-five stores, five saloons, and three hotels. By 1865 there was a newspaper, called the *Columbia Press* — later the *Umatilla Press.*

Along the routes leading from The Dalles to Umatilla Landing, and from the landing to the mines of the interior, roadhouses furnished food and lodging. They also had livery stables for the horses. Men began operating toll ferries and bridges along the way. Merchants followed, then blacksmiths and saloonkeepers, and mining towns sprang to life. When the post office arrived, the town added respectability and, in many cases, a name.

Homesteaders filed on the surrounding land. It was easy to tell the difference between a mining town and one founded by homesteaders, for there were women and children in the homestead village. The early-day miners were nearly all single, or men with families back home, and the first women in the mining camps were usually camp followers. Churches and schools were established in the farming communities. The miner, footloose and fancy free, preferred to receive his spiritual welfare from a bottle.

In 1862 only five cabins stood in the beautiful Grande Ronde Valley; they were clustered together for protection against the Indians. Ten men, two women, and eight children resided in this tiny settlement, called Brown's Town, where Ben Brown ran a trading post. Just one year later a thriving community was growing there, settled by many of the thousands passing through on their way to the mines. The fertile soil was just what the homesteaders were looking for. In 1863 a post office was established and the name was changed to La Grande. It was soon a booming town with two newspapers — the *Blue Mountain Times* and the *Grande Ronde Sentinel,* both established in 1868.

The rapid growth of La Grande was typical of many towns along the roads leading to the goldfields. Like many other towns, La Grande continued to grow as new mines were opened.

The flow of gold had lessened and the down-river shipments of grain increased by the time the Harvest Queen was put into operation. She was an elaborate boat that lost nothing in beauty because of her versatile utility. The Queen, as she was called, was capable of carrying a huge cargo of grain. The building in the background is the famous Umatilla House.

Shearers Bridge is a few miles east of Tygh Valley. Joe Shearer was one of the early-day packers along the trail between The Dalles and Canyon City. In 1871, he paid John Todd $7,041 for his make-shift bridge across The Deschutes River. He built a new bridge and improved the roads for 30 miles on each side of the river. Shearer built a 13-room hotel and restaurant. He charged 25¢ for a meal and $3.75 a team and wagon to cross the bridge.

To follow the sequence of events in eastern Oregon's gold stampede, it is necessary to drop back to The Dalles and another rush to goldfields two hundred miles south of there. In June 1862 the precious metal was found at Canyon City — in great quantity and almost on the surface. Hundreds of men and pack animals left The Dalles every day, traveling south along a poorly blazed trail marked by the army.

For the first two years it remained merely a trail, with few places along the way to accommodate weary travelers. Then in 1864 it was widened into a wagon road. The first stage from The Dalles to Canyon City made the trip in May of that year. The driver was Henry Wheeler, for whom Wheeler County is named. He drove a Concord stage powered by a four-horse hitch and carrying eleven passengers, each paying $40 for one-way passage. Teams were changed at eight relay stations along the way, and meals were served at each stop.

Wheeler received $12,000 a year from the government for carrying the mail, plus a fee from Wells Fargo Express. He was once shot in a raid by Indians but managed to escape. They took his horses, then cut all the leather from the stagecoach. Not knowing paper money value, they scattered $10,000 in currency to the wind.

Thousands of people traveled this lonely trail, many camping off the road at night to avoid danger. Because of the great wealth moving from Canyon City to The Dalles, guarding a pack train from highwaymen and marauding Indians was dangerous business. Nearly a thousand white people were killed by Indians in mining country, first by Chief Paulina and his roving bands and

In the early 1800s Berry Wey was convicted of murder and sentenced to hang. He was tried by a miners' jury, loaded into a hack and seated on a pine box which was to serve as his coffin. The gallows were built on the summit of the hill near the present cemetery. Just before Berry was hung, he said, "I don't want to die with my boots on, boys. Can I take them off?" On his grave rested a pair of well-worn boots.

Courtesy Oregon Historical Society

The distance from The Dalles to Canyon City was 197 miles. There were eight relay stations along the way and the stages made the trip in three days. The charge was $40 per person. This type of stage was called a mud wagon.

Twelve horses and mules, 2 wagons loaded with supplies, on the road from The Dalles to Canyon City; mule skinner riding wheel horse.

Courtesy Oregon Historical Society

Bakeoven is south of the Sherman County Line, 50 miles southeast of The Dalles and eight miles northwest of Shaniko. At one time it had a Post Office, general store, hotel and blacksmith shop and was on the road from The Dalles to Canyon City. In the early mining days a Frenchman traveling with a packtrain loaded with flour destined for Canyon City camped overnight at this point. That night the Indians drove off his mules leaving the packer stranded with his bags of flour. He did not despair. He gathered rocks, built an oven, then sat there day after day, baking bread and selling it to the passing miners, making a greater profit than he could have made from the raw flour.

And that is how Bakeoven received its name.

later, in what was known as the Bannock War, by the braves of Chief Buffalo Horn and Egan.

One of the early-day road agents was Jim Berriway, later known as Barry-Way. Somewhere along the trail from Canyon City to The Dalles his gang murdered John Galliger, a pack train operator. Berriway fled to the mines in Idaho but was returned by the vigilantes to Canyon City, where he

soon dangled at the end of a rope. His skull and the rope used to hang him are exhibited in the Grant County Museum in Canyon City.

Another outlaw named Gallon was "hung by the neck until dead." The local newspaper ran this headline, "One Drop and a Gallon Less."

Along a trail leading to the mines in Idaho, a packer named Welch was robbed of his gold dust. Welch said, "I'll see you again." The robber replied, "No you won't." Then he blew Welch's head off with a double-barreled shotgun. The trails needed protection from such brutality, and the cleanup came with miners' law and the vigilantes — who took over as they had done in the early days of mining in southern Oregon. Between 1863 and 1865, thirty-two outlaws died at the hands of the vigilantes along the route to Oregon and Idaho mines.[48]

Millions of dollars in gold poured from the mines at Auburn and Canyon City and from the diggings in Idaho and was sent on its way to the San Francisco mint. The charge from the mines to The Dalles was

The Sierra Nevada from August 24, 1862 to December 2, 1864 carried $2 million in gold dust from Portland to the Mint in San Francisco. The Sierra Nevada was only one of many ships carrying gold from Oregon to the Mint.

Courtesy Oregon Historical Society

three and one-quarter percent of the weight. From The Dalles and upriver ports the treasure traveled by riverboat to Portland, and then to San Francisco on ocean steamers.

Later still, shipments were made by mail. Flat tin cans were used, sealed with solder. A heavy manila envelope took care of several cans, with a maximum weight of 250 ounces. No records are available on how much gold moved by mail. No doubt it was considerable, as it proved to be cheaper.[49]

Shipping records aren't complete, but the following steamship listings and Wells Fargo Express shipments indicate the enormous quantity of gold coming from the mines east of the Cascade Mountains. The steamship records are available for only the first four years, 1861 through 1864; the Wells Fargo records cover the period 1864 through 1867.[50] In all cases the shipments are Portland to San Francisco:

Date	Steamer	Amount
Oct. 11, 1861	Pacific	$172,904
Dec. 12, 1861	Pacific	141,820
Aug. 5, 1862	Tenino	200,000
Aug. 24, 1862	Sierra Nevada	195,000
Oct. 27, 1862	Sierra Nevada	500,000
Sept. 24, 1863	Brother Jonathan	315,000
Oct. 5, 1863	Sierra Nevada	236,761
Oct. 12, 1863	Brother Jonathan	203,835
Nov. 13, 1863	Sierra Nevada	500,000
Dec. 4, 1863	Oregon	750,000
June 2, 1864	Oregon	330,000
June 27, 1864	John L. Stephens	515,649
July 5, 1864	Pacific	213,899
Aug. 3, 1864	Oregon	321,000
Aug. 21, 1864	Pacific	366,465
Dec. 2, 1864	Sierra Nevada	517,250
Oct. 28, 1864	Brother Jonathan	500,000
Nov. 5, 1864	Brother Jonathan	339,000
Total		$6,318,583

Wells Fargo Express:

Date	Amount
1864	$6,200,000
1865	5,800,000
1866	5,400,000
1867	4,001,000
Total	$21,401,000

Canyon City fire April 19, 1937 — looking east from highway

Courtesy Oliver Historical Museum

BIG STRIKE IN WHISKEY GULCH

CANYON CITY'S RICH DISCOVERY was made by a group of California miners on their way to the new gold strike at Auburn. They camped the evening of June 7, 1862 on a clear stream near the John Day River. Next morning William A. Allard struck gold that panned out $18 to $20 a pan. It has been estimated that $26,000,000 was taken from this one small canyon — the richest single placer diggings in Oregon.

Professor J. Waldemar Lindgren, the eminent geologist, estimated in 1901[51] that between $3,000,000 and $5,000,000 a year were taken from Canyon Creek for the first three years. Rossiter W. Raymond, U.S. Commissioner of Mining Statistics, lent support by saying that from 1865 to 1870 the area produced an average of $22,000 a week, or about $1,144,000 a year. Then came a gradual tapering off for a number of years, dropping to $100,000.[52] The land between Canyon City and John Day, now known as Humbolt Drive, was once priced at $500 a square yard. The ground was so rich a single pan produced as much as $150 (about seven ounces of gold).

It was said that Canyon Creek was first called Whiskey Gulch because the ground was so rich the water was reserved for mining — whiskey was plentiful, and a shortage of water was no handicap.

Untold millions were taken from the virgin ground in the mines east of the Cascades — "untold" because no government records of gold production were kept for the first eighteen years. During the peak of the Can-

yon City rush, claims were filed at the rate of one every few minutes. The first claim was filed on July 7, 1862. Within a year, close to 5,000 people worked along the gulch and another 5,000 in the upper valley.

The first miners into Canyon City were followed by the usual gamblers, dance hall girls, and saloonkeepers. The first saloon was in a tent, with a barrel of "rot gut" whiskey and a few tin cups. Tents were soon replaced by cabins, and within a few months Canyon City had several general stores, twelve saloons, and a sizable boot hill. The main street was so narrow a team of horses couldn't turn around.

There were homesteaders as well as miners. The first families to arrive overland from California came from near Red Bluff. They reached Canyon City late in 1862. In this train were 32 wagons, 105 men, 14 women, and a few children.

The townsite was laid out on July 20, 1862; the post office opened in April 1864. That same year, Grant County was carved from Wasco. Canyon City was named county seat, and the proud citizens built the Old Pioneer Courthouse. It wasn't until 1891 that Canyon City was incorporated, with C. W. Parrish elected mayor.

Charles Becker and Peter Zimmerman operated the first store, in a log cabin. Prices were high, everything having arrived by pack mule from The Dalles. John Herberger raised and sold potatoes at twenty-five cents a pound, with a limit of four pounds per customer. Large potatoes were

Courtesy Oregon Historical Society

A miners' meeting in the Canyon City district during the early mining days. There are 178 men in this picture. Note that the majority are young men; not the movie type of the typical old man with long white whiskers and a big floppy hat following a burro. A packtrain is in the background.

Native gold in leaf-and-wire form as received directly from lode sources.

Harold McCall photograph

Gold nuggets came in all shapes and forms. Note the round polished one that looks like a button. (U.S National Bank, Baker, Oregon)

Canyon City, Oregon about 1898 before the bad fire of November 11, 1898. No. 1 would be about where museum now stands; No. 2 would be present location Gail's Market; and No. 3 footbridge going to courthouse.

Gold scales at the museum as Canyon City. Twenty-six million dollars came from this area, no doubt these old scales could tell an interesting story.

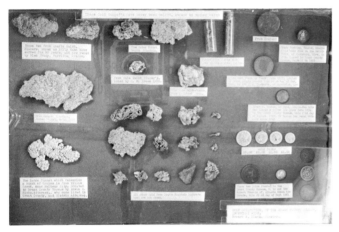

Canyon City gold display at Grant County Museum, Canyon City, Oregon.

Courtesy Grant County Museum

Hon. Charles W. Parrish, a prominent attorney, and Canyon City's first mayor.

four for a dollar. Some of the early-day prices were:

Can of pepper, 75 cents; bar of soap, $1.00; one-half gallon of coal oil, $2.50; small keg of syrup, $18.75; tea, $1.50 tin; oysters, $1.25 can; and miner's gold pan, $3.00. At one time flour sold for 55 cents a pound; beans, 50 cents a pound; pair of blankets, $25; cigar, 50 cents. The saloon-keeper received his whiskey by pack mule; two small kegs made a load for a mule, and he carried his burden 200 miles over a rough trail. The thirsty miner dug deep into his poke to sooth his parched throat.

Canyon City had its colorful characters such as R. H. J. Comer, the first Oregon newspaper editor east of The Dalles. He came to town in 1868 with his job press and sacks of lead. The office furniture consisted of a few dry-goods boxes. He called his three-column newspaper *The City Journal*. In his column "Our Say" Comer stated: "Local news being of such nature that everybody knows every other's business except his own, we shall publish only such as suits our purpose."[53]

G. I. Hazeltine, one of the first miners to arrive in Canyon City following the gold strike in 1862. His mine was located right in the center of where the town of John Day stands today. He established the first flour mill in John Day. History records him as the first photographer in the area and his pictures are collector's items.

Courtesy Grant County Museum

B. C. Trowbridge came to John Day and Canyon City in 1862. Located the first homestead in Grant County. His gold came from farming the rich valley land.

Goods were scarce, so the merchants found no need to advertise. Consequently, Comer was broke and forced to work his mining claim. But he kept his humor. One day he wrote in his paper, "Mr. Comer, our printer, is out prospecting. I hope he makes it, for no man is more deserving."

The preacher found himself in much the same position as Comer. He had something to sell but few takers, for gold was the miner's god. Most preachers were obliged to work for wages in the mines during the week then preach in the street on Sunday.

In 1864 another personality arrived in Canyon City, along with his wife, a few head of cattle, and a license to practice law. Tied to his saddle were a few small apple trees. He was Cincinnatus Hiner Miller, later known as Joaquin Miller, the poet. To Miller goes the honor for planting the first orchard east of The Dalles. He was a rabid Secessionist and had left Eugene, Oregon, after the government suppressed his news-

paper there, refusing him permission to send it through the mail.

Miller was an admirer of the poet Byron, imitating him even to the limp. His hair was long and white, and he wore high boots with one trouser tucked in and a Prince Albert coat with a velvet collar just like Byron's. Miller practiced law and became county

Courtesy Grant County Museum

Mr. H. L. Sells seated fourth from right in front of his brewery. He came to Canyon City during the gold rush in the early 1860s. He was active in the Prairie Diggings, a rich mine between Prairie City and John Day.

Wesley Andrews photograph

Baker-Canyon stage near Austin, Oregon 1909

Courtesy Oregon Historical Society

St. Thomas Episcopal Church at Canyon City built in 1876. The first church in the county. The ornate windows were shipped around the Horn. Two fires burned Canyon City to the ground but each time the old church was spared. St. Thomas was built when Canyon City was a rough mining town where the citizens were more interested in saloons and in gold than Salvation. The first service was held in the church on July 11, 1877.

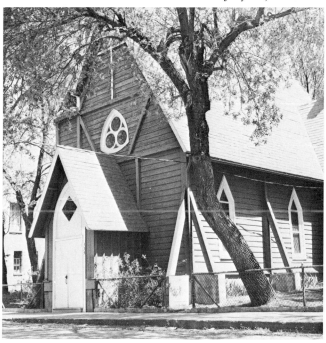

judge. After leaving Canyon City he sometimes represented himself as an old-time prospector. Tiring of this role, he became an Indian fighter. His ability as a poet is questionable, although one of his three wives was a fine poet. (Another wife was Indian.) His Canyon City cabin is now at the Grant County Museum.

George I. Hazeltine, an excellent photographer, arrived in Canyon City in 1862. A few of his pictures appear in this book, taken from glass-plate negatives more than a hundred years old. H. L. Sells owned the brewery and was Justice of the Peace from 1864 to 1866.

When the gold played out, the miners moved on, their names lost forever. But those who turned to business and farming have descendants among the area's most prominent citizens. Joe C. Oliver, B. C. Trowbridge, Charles Belshaw, John Herberger—all helped build Grant County and all have descendants who are respected stockmen and businessmen today.

In 1895 in front of the old news office in Canyon City,
Oregon; moving boiler to Vance Creek.

Old-timer and his mine near Canyon City

Both Canyon City and John Day had picturesque Chinatowns, complete with joss
house, restaurants, laundries, and a
Chinese doctor who was highly respected
by both races. In the mines, however, the
history of the Chinese was much the same
as in southern Oregon.

Discrimination against Orientals in the
mines started in 1851. At that time Oregon
law read: "No Chinaman not a resident of
the State at the time of the adoption of this
Constitution shall ever hold real estate or
work for himself any mining claim
therein."[54] They could only work for wages
— usually twenty-five cents for a ten-hour
day.

Under certain conditions and restrictions,
Chinese were later allowed to occupy
ground, but they were taxed $4.00 a month,
payable in advance every three months.
Any Oriental found mining without a
license was liable to have his property taken
from him and sold at an hour's notice. The
laws were amended several times, but sel-
dom to the advantage of the Chinese.

Not until the 1880s, after the white man
had skimmed the cream, were restrictions
relaxed; then two-thirds of the placer mining was done by Chinese, who made a liv-

Joaquin Miller's home in Canyon
City. His real name was Cincinnatus
Hiner Miller. The poet came to Canyon City during the gold rush after the
government closed his newspaper in
Eugene, Oregon. He was a colorful
figure who became county judge in
Grant County. He has the honor of
having planted the first fruit trees east
of The Dalles.

Congregational Church, one of the first churches east of The Dalles; old building still standing

The Elkhorn Hotel, Canyon City, Oregon, Walter Fields, proprietor, J. C. Oliver's milkwagon in front, about 1908. Joe Oliver came not to mine but to farm. He was very successful. His sons are highly respected businessmen and stockmen in Grant County today.

ing from ground abandoned by the white miners.

Each mining town has its colorful past recorded in its local newspaper, and Canyon City is no exception. In 1889 Orin S.

Patterson started the *Blue Mountain Eagle.* Many an interesting story like this one about "Old Brigham" may be found in the files.

Brigham was an old-time miner who loved to gamble; with him, a little cheating was all right. One night he was caught taking a few chips from the table that were not rightfully his. Quick as a flash, the owner whipped out a Spanish dagger. When the excitement was over, one of Brigham's fingers was left beside the pilfered chips.[55]

Canyon City today is a clean little town. It has experienced three disastrous fires over the years. Each time, before the ashes cooled, a new Canyon City has sprung to life. St. Thomas Episcopal Church, one of the most beautiful in the West, has survived all three fires. Much of the material for the church was shipped around Cape Horn.

The citizens of Grant County take pride in preserving reminders of the past in their fine museum. It is a place to take your children, lest they forget their forefathers who laid the foundation for all that we have today.

TIGER TOWN AND OTHER CAMPS

JOHN DAY'S HISTORY IS CLOSELY RELATED to that of Canyon City. They are twin towns: when you mention one, you could be talking about the other.

Back when gold was discovered at Canyon City, John Day was called Tiger Town. At one time Canyon City, was known as Upper Town and John Day as Lower Town. The name finally became John Day. The post office, first opened in 1865, was discontinued in 1871, and for eight years all mail came to Canyon City. In 1879 the town again had its own post office, with Frank I. McCullum as postmaster.

At one time G. I. Hazeltine, P. V. Middlesworth, and C. B. Cobb operated placer mines on the very spot where the business section stands today. E. B. Fearing owned the first general store, Shorty Mosier the first saloon, and Charles Cobb the first hotel. In 1881 John Day had two general stores, two small hotels, two livery stables, a harness shop, a flour mill, two blacksmith shops, and three "secret orders" — lodges, we call them today.

When fire destroyed the Chinese section in Canyon City in 1885 the citizens refused to let the Orientals rebuild, so they moved down to Tiger Town. At the peak, one thousand whites and an equal number of Chinese were living there.

John Day became an incorporated city on June 7, 1900, and over the years gradually grew into the chief trading center in the Upper John Day River Valley, although Canyon City is still the county seat.

The Kam Wah Chung Company building still stands, a monument to the past when there were as many Orientals in the town as whites. Dr. Ing Hay and Lung On established the company years ago. Dr. Hay was a herbologist, and many white people up and down the river preferred him to a regular medical doctor. Lung On, known locally as Leon, died in 1940, Dr. Hay about 1950.

The City of John Day now owns the building and is considering turning it into a museum. When an inspection was made of the building's contents, officials found quantities of Dr. Hay's strange herbs, plants, and such things as dried bear claws, dried beetles, shrimp, pickled rattlesnakes, opium, and opium pipes. (It was legal to import opium into the United States until 1905, in brass tins with U.S. revenue stamps attached.) Near the chimney a false floor was discovered where seventy-two bottles of bourbon whiskey distilled in 1913 had been stored.

The first strike in the valley above John Day was called the Prairie Diggins'. It was about three miles east of town and for a time was the richest mine in the area. It has been said that the first miners averaged as high as $2,000 an hour. There were eighteen original owners, and each cleaned up $10,000 the first year. Later a 25-stamp mill was installed, employing forty men.[56]

On Little Pine Creek between John Day and Prairie City another strike was made. The camp was called Marysville, and it

Courtesy Oregon Historical Society

A very early picture of John Day, supposedly a Hazeltine photo

A poor picture but an interesting one of an early-day barbecue at John Day

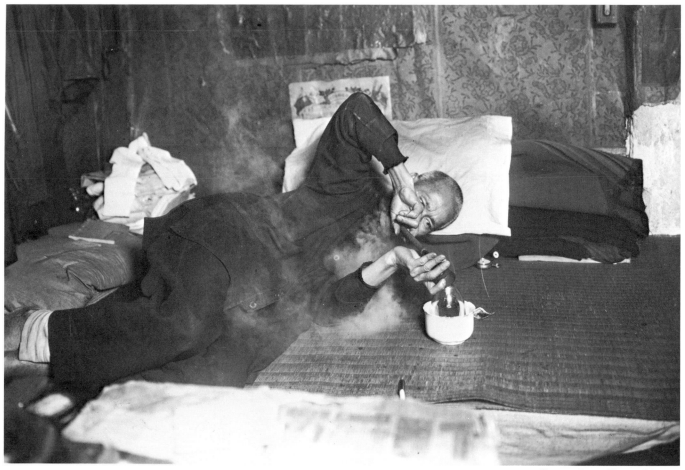

Courtesy Oregon Historical Society

A chinese opium smoker. Many of the old-time Orientals who came to this country in the early days were hooked on the habit. In fact, it was legal to import opium into the U.S. until 1905.

This building in John Day was the headquarters of the 600 Chinese in the John Day Valley who were left after the gold dwindled out in Canyon City. It is still standing today, and was built about 1866. The firm Kam Wah Chung Company carried authentic Chinese merchandise including food, medicine, fine silk and china, firecrackers, and opium. This was also headquarters for the famous Chinese doctor, Doc Hay, who saved the lives of many people throughout the years.

The Prairie Diggins Mine was located three miles east of John Day toward Prairie City and was reported to be very rich. It was owned by a group of Canyon City men including Mr. Sells, the owner of the brewery.

Courtesy Grant County Museum

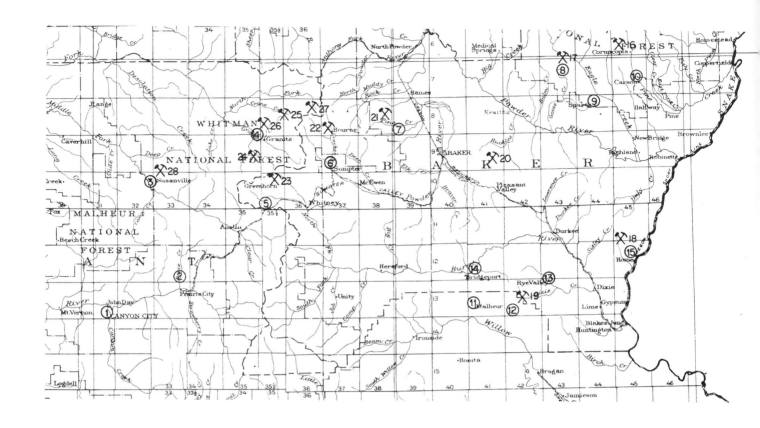

GOLD MINES OF THE BLUE MOUNTAINS OF OREGON

Placer mines

1. Canyon Creek
2. Dixie Creek
3. Susanville
4. Granite
5. Whitney
6. Sumpter
7. Auburn-Pocahontas
8. Sanger
9. Sparta
10. Carson-Pine Creek
11. Malheur-Eldorado
12. Mormon Basin
13. Rye Valley
14. Bridgeport
15. Conner Creek

Lode mines

16. Cornucopia
17. Sanger
18. Conner Creek
19. Rainbow
20. Virtue
21. Baisley-Elkhorn
22. North Pole-Columbia lode
23. Bonanza
24. Red Boy
25. Buffalo
26. Cougar-Independence
27. LaBellvue
28. Badger

One of the early day lode mines near Canyon City

Prairie City is old but not a mining town; the city fathers made sure of that by finding the ground non-mineral. Dixietown was just up the creek a short way and it was here that $1,000,000 was taken from the gravel on Dixie Creek. When the miners who owned the land started digging under the buildings, it was time for the city dudes to move; and that was when Prairie City was born.

boomed for a short time. Today not even a board remains.

Another strike was at Dixie Town, on rich placer ground a short distance from the present site of Prairie City. Between three and four hundred people worked the mine, and the take has been reported at $1,000,000. There were two general stores at Dixie Town, one owned by H. H. Hyde and the other by George Dolling. Jules Le Brent operated the livery stable. W. M. Davis ran one of the two hotels.

The town stood on a gravel bar owned by a group of miners. When these gentlemen began digging under the buildings, the townspeople thought it was time to move. A new site was laid out, and this time the citizens made sure there was no gold in the ground where they relocated! They called the new town Prairie City. It received its post office in 1870 and was incorporated February 18, 1891.

The *Prairie City Miner* was among the early-day newspapers in Grant County; Clinton P. Haight was its pioneer editor. In 1910 Prairie City became the terminus of the narrow-gauge Sumpter Valley Railway from Baker City. When hard-rock mining came into its own, a post office was opened at Comer near the head of Dixie Creek. The

office served both Dixie Meadow and the Quartzburg areas.

As soon as an area was mined out, the prospectors moved on, this time across the divide and down the Middle Fork of the John Day River. Each little stream along the Middle Fork had hordes of men panning

The Dixie Meadows mine is located in the Quartzburg district in Grant County, Sections 23 and 24, T.11S.R.33E., near the head of Ruby Creek just north of the Dixie Creek Divide.

Courtesy Grant County Museum

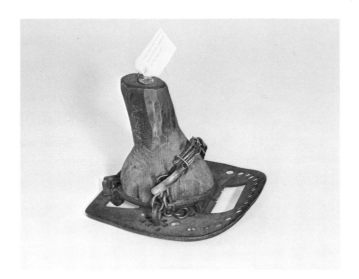

and sluicing for gold, and the creeks ran thick with mud. A new strike was made at Susanville on Elk Creek in 1864 by a party of California prospectors. Today not even a ghost is left, but it was a rip-roaring camp in its day. The gravel along Elk Creek was so rich and the gulch so narrow that the local mining rules stated *"a placer claim across the gulch shall be no wider than the distance the miner can reach with his pick handle."* This led to the story that Susan-

A snowshoe used on horses during the deep
snow of winter.

Pioneer woman in front of her homestead cabin in the winter's first snow in the upper John
Day Valley in the 1860s.

A *Hazeltine photograph*   *Courtesy Oregon Historical Society*

U.S. branding iron found at the site of abandoned old Fort Harney.

The Pomeroy Dredge in operation below the town of John Day. Dredging was the fastest way of working placer gravels, and after 1913, produced more gold in Oregon that all all other processes combined. The dredges worked from 1,000 to 1,500 yards of gravel per day.

ville miners had the longest pick handles in the world.

The Cabell Mine on Elk Creek yielded $88,000 from a little hole seventy feet deep. Both placer and hard-rock mining were carried on here for a number of years. When the white men left, the Chinese continued. The old town of Galena stands today on what was once the site of Susanville's post office.

The Badger Mine discovered in 1865 was one of the first quartz mines in eastern Oregon. The owners used an old-fashioned Spanish arrastra for grinding the ore. Several other fine quartz mines were in the

district, among them The Mammoth, Stockton, Bull of the Woods, Gem, Skyscraper, Princess, Ophir, and Mayflower. Of the group, the Badger was the best known. Thirty-seven men worked the mine, bonded in 1897 for $8,000. Within a year four hundred tons of ore shipped to the smelter returned $60,000.[57]

The small, but rich, Great Northern Mine, on the north side of Canyon Mountain, near Canyon City in Grant County, was discovered by Ike Guker, standing in the center. Man on right standing on the bank is Frank McBean, old-time stage driver to Winnemucca. It is known that Guker let visitors pick nuggets and keep them. There was $65,000 taken from this little hole. The mine was discovered as late as 1897.

Courtesy Grant County Museum

The Elk Creek placers near Susanville were worked over many times. The gravels were rich and produced an untold amount of gold. The Chinese were the last to work there and they made a living on what the white man left.

A McCord photograph

The Badger Mine near Susanville was a gold mine discovered in the very early days and was one of the most productive.

A McCord photograph

Arrastra used for grinding ore to release the gold. This one was water powered. The Arrastra was the forerunner of the modern stamp mill and was first used in Mexico. This one was located one-quarter mile below Susanville, Oregon.

When both placer and quartz mining slowed down, dredges started operating along the Middle Fork of the John Day. The total take from all operations is said to have been close to $1,000,000.

Many of Oregon's largest gold nuggets came from this area. The Buck Creek placers, three miles north of Galena, were noted for fine nugget specimens. The Armstrong Nugget, now on display at the U.S. National Bank of Oregon in Baker, came from here.

The following was notarized in Baker in 1903 — a placer miner's experience near Susanville:

The undersigned, being first duly sworn, herewith certifies that in the spring of 1883, he and his partner started work on a bedrock flume on what were considered exhausted placer diggings on Elk Creek near Susanville, Grant County, Oregon; that up to 1892, while doing preparatory work, they managed to make expenses and that thereafter the extraction of gold dust and nuggets was as follows:

1893	$13,843
1894	10,587
1895	6,056
1896	4,520
1897	4,318
1898	22,311
1899	8,041

Number of men employed was from six to ten during a season of six and one-half months in each year.

The total expense during the seven years was in the neighborhood of $35,000, leaving a net profit of about $35,000 out of supposedly worked-out, valueless, and abandoned placer claims; and they are being profitably operated at this time.

(Signed) N. C. HASKELL

Sworn to before me, a Notary Public, this 3rd day of March, 1903. Fred R. Mellis, Notary Public for Oregon.[57]

As fast as streams along the Middle Fork of the John Day River were staked, other miners pressed onward and upward into the Green-Horn Mountains. This range is actually a part of the Blue Mountains, the snow-capped summit forming an east-west ridge that divides the Middle and North forks of the John Day. The highest point is known as Vinegar Hill — elevation 8,131 feet.

Vinegar Hill became the center of the eastern Oregon goldfields as early as 1863. There are references to Green-Horn in early letters and mining papers. Old-timers, describing the location of their properties, would say their mine was so many miles from the Green-Horn — referring to a beautiful monolith of green serpentine rock more than 300 feet high, standing at the head of Salmon Creek. It is almost in the center of the mining district. (The area was not surveyed until the 1880s by the United States, so there were no townships or sections to refer to.)

The Green-Horn Mountains received their name from the huge serpentine rock. But somewhere along the line the little hyphen was carelessly dropped, and for many years the mountains have been called Greenhorn, changing the meaning of the name entirely. Unfortunately, the new spelling has passed into such general use that one is almost compelled to accept it.

The huge rock or monolith in the foreground is at the 7,500 foot level on Vinegar Butte. It is over 300 feet high and formed of solid green serpentine. In the early mining days, the old sourdough use it as a landmark and they called it the GREEN-HORN. The Greenhorn Mountains received their name from this huge rock. It is located at the head of Salmon Creek in Section 7, T102,R35E.

Placer Miner's Experience

The undersigned, being first duly sworn, herewith certifies that in the Spring of 1883, he and his partner started work on a bedrock flume on what were considered exhausted placer diggings, on Elk Creek near Susanville, Grant County, Oregon ; that up to 1892, while doing preparatory work, they managed to make expenses and that after that the extraction of gold dust and nuggets was as follows :

1893	$13,843.00
1894	10,587.00
1895	6,056.00
1896	4,520.00
1897	4,318.00
1898	22,311.00
1899	8,041.00

Number of men employed was from six to ten during a season of 6½ months in each year.

The total expense during the seven years was in the neighborhood of $35,000, leaving a net profit of about $35,000, out of supposedly worked out, valueless, and abandoned placer claims. Since then we have disposed of the claims at a good price, and they are being operated profitably at this time.

(*Signed*) N. C. HASKELL.

Sworn to before me, a Notary Public, this 3d day of March, A. D. 1903.

FRED R. MELLIS,
Notary Public for Oregon.

Placer Miner's Experience on Elk Creek near Susanville, Oregon.

FORTUNE HUNTERS INVADE THE MOUNTAINS

ROBINSONVILLE, IN GRANT COUNTY, one mile east of Greenhorn, was the first town established in the Greenhorn Mountains. Following the Canyon City strikes, fortune hunters by the thousands moved to new discoveries. In 1864 a group of men on the headwaters of Olive Creek high in the Greenhorn Mountains uncovered rich deposits of gold in rotten quartz, almost on the surface. These men were too busy staking claims, setting up tents, and building cabins to think of building a town.

The first man to strike gold was William Daggett, who later became Robinsonville's first and only postmaster. Strangely, the town wasn't named for him, as was sometimes the case. The honor went to William Robinson, who arrived in the busy mining camp with his companion, " '49 Jimmy" Gavin, in 1868. Robinsonville's post office was the first on the mountain — opening a month before the one in John Day. There were also two general stores, a blacksmith shop, livery stable, two saloons, a hotel, and a boardinghouse. At the edge of town was a cabin with a madam in charge. If a school was established, there is no record of it. During the boom period, two daily stages served the community.

A story in the *Sumpter News* in April 1899 stated that 1,200 people resided in Robinsonville. The *Morning Democrat* of Baker City said in the 1880s that Robinsonville once had a population of 5,000. Several years of research do not bear this out. The U.S. Post Office Department states that

about 1,000 people received mail there. That seems reasonable, since Robinsonville was the only post office on the mountain, and there were mines everywhere. A more realistic population for the town would be in the neighborhood of 400.

As with most mining communities, when surface or placer mining began to slow down, many rich veins had been uncovered below the surface, so attention was turned to underground or quartz mining. Some quartz mines furnished employment for a number of men. One was the Virginian, where a $70,000 pocket was uncovered. Other mines close to Robinsonville were the Morning Glory, Phoenix, Don Juan, I.X.L., Worley, Humbolt, Black Hawk, Rabbit, Golden Gate, Gold Coin, Golden Eagle, Pyx, Red Bird, Owl, and Royal White. This same group of mines was later served by the town of Greenhorn.

One night in 1884 Robinsonville burned to the ground, sparing only a few houses at the edge of the business area. One of the saved homes belonged to '49 Jimmy. Gavin had followed the California gold rush trails in 1849, and that's how he became known as '49 Jimmy. He arrived at Robinsonville in 1864 and lived there the rest of his life. The district's richest mine, the Bonanza, was only four and a half miles away, yet he never got that far from home in thirty-seven years.

When Jimmy grew old and ill he refused to leave his house so friends carried water, chopped wood, and kept him in food. He lived alone with his rooster Jim, his cat Tab,

Picture on left is old-time miner's oil lamp; in the center is a candle mould and at right a home-made iron.

Mrs. Johanna Elliott, wife of David Elliott, came to Robinsonville about 1868.

Elliot Family photograph

Mr. Otis J. Elliott was born in Robinsonville during the gold rush. He lived his entire life in Baker County. Mr. Elliott was a highly respected and successful stockman.

Wm. Steward photograph

Election board precinct Number 20, Grant County, Robinsonville, Oregon. Left to right: Harry Stevenson, Bob Butler, Frank Steward, Pearl Steward, William Steward inside Stevenson cabin; now owned by George Childers in John Day, Oregon.

The Virginia Mine is located one and one-half miles northeast of the town of Greenhorn in Grant County, near the old townsite of Robinsonville. Old records state that a $70,000 pocket of gold, so rich it looked like nut candy, came from this old mine.

A McCord photograph

The Don Juan Mill and Mine near Greenhorn, Oregon

Phoenix Mill and Mine, near Greenhorn, Oregon

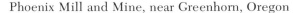

Wm. Steward photograph
Superintendent's cabin at Phoenix Mine on headwaters of Burnt River; a 10-stamp mill operated 24 hours a day. The ore ran $36 a ton but did not hold up in depth.

Working a windless at the Phoenix Mine

"49" Jimmie came to Robinsonville in the early 1860s from the mines in California. He was a small man who they say could swear in seven different languages. Jimmie lived alone with Tab, his cat; Jim, his rooster; and Victoria, a hen. The chickens roosted on the rafters inside his little one-room cabin.

"49" Jimmie's cabin at Robinsonville, Oregon

and his hen Victoria. In 1901, when he was 77, he became helpless and was moved to the "poorhouse," as it was then called. A short time later the old fellow died. He was the last inhabitant of Robinsonville, a composite of all his comrades — bighearted and rough of speech. (They say he could swear in seven languages.)

A few years after his death, stories began to circulate that '49 Jimmy had been a rich man and a miser, that his money was buried somewhere around his cabin. Soon the walls of the cabin were torn down and the surrounding ground dug up as though it had been plowed.

There is no record of what happened to Jim, Tab, and Victoria. They and the town have vanished, leaving behind only barren earth.[58]

THE SAGA OF GREENHORN

OLD GREENHORN IS ONE TOWN you will not find in your history books. Yet in early mining days, around 1870, two to three hundred people lived in and around the town, the second in the Greenhorn Mountains.

It was the highest town in Oregon at the time, with an elevation of 7,500 feet. It was about two miles northwest of the present lookout on Vinegar Butte (Vinegar Hill) and about three-quarters of a mile southeast of Dupratt Springs. Old Greenhorn existed only a short time and never had a post office; it lived and died at least ten years before the present town of Greenhorn City was born. A number of rich gold and silver mines were worked in the area, but the winters were extremely severe and the snow was twelve to fourteen feet deep. The founders were tough men but not that tough, and it soon became a ghost town.

The buildings were all on one street. The only connection with the outside world was a road of sorts that followed the divide to Indian Rock, then down Desolation Creek in the direction of Heppner and The Dalles. A few shipments of high-grade ore were made by wagon and pack mule, but it was a lost cause from the start, since Robinsonville was only a few miles to the southeast. No historical mention is made of this old town, named for the huge rock known as the Green-Horn.

Greenhorn City is a rock hound and bottle hunters' delight, with a ghost under every boulder. It is the highest (6,271 feet) and smallest incorporated town in Oregon. Greenhorn is so high that nine different mill whistles can be heard on a clear day.

In the early 1970s property owners reactivated the charter, making the historic camp a full-fledged, legally incorporated city with an elected mayor (who happens to be this author) and other city officials. This was done primarily for protection against land speculators who might turn the colorful old camp into a tourist area with gaudy donut shops and hamburger stands. The present owners enjoy the beauty, solitude, and rich history of the old mining town and don't want it spoiled by modern "progress."

The town was born during a period when surface or placer mining was slowing down, and hard-rock or lode mining was getting under way. The Forest Service historical marker on Main Street gives 1891 as the year the city was founded. The newspaper *Long Creek Eagle* reported at the time that thirty-two cabins were on the site, with an average of three persons to a cabin. In 1884 Robinsonville, a mile to the east, had burned to the ground. It was never rebuilt, and the more suitable site at Greenhorn grew like Topsy. A post office was opened in 1902, with Burton Miller as postmaster.

About this time, Simeon C. Richardson arrived in Greenhorn. With the help of E. G. Stephenson, he established law and order in the rip-roaring mining camp. They petitioned the state legislature to have the town incorporated, and this was granted on

The I.X.L. Mine is located just east of the town of Greenhorn on the head of Lightning Creek. It was owned by Fred J. Kelly of Boise, Idaho for many years. The mine was 300 feet deep and equipped with a modern quartz mill. The prospects were good, but pumps were necessary to keep the mine from flooding. Tempska, a form of fossilized fern or palm, is found here. This is the only known place in the United States where this variety is found. Hundreds of people come to this area each year in search for the rare fossil.

The I.X.L. Mine near the town of Greenhorn; office on left; boarding house on right.

A McCord photograph

The I.X.L. Mine near the town of Greenhorn. The man on the left is Fred J. Kelly, owner and developer of several mines in the district. His home was in Boise, Idaho.

The I.X.L. Mine mill and cyanide plant near the town of Greenhorn.

Old circular saw used to cut lumber in the early mining days in the Robinsonville area. NOTE: There are only eight teeth on saw. The lady is Verna Gilliland who has mined in the area for many years.

The Humbolt Mine near Greenhorn was known as a pocket mine and successfully worked with water from the Pete Mann ditch. Harold McCall of Oregon City owns the mine.

The Black Hawk Mine, one and one-half miles north of the town of Greenhorn, now owned by Ray Myers of Baker, Oregon

In 1912, the mining town of Greenhorn, Oregon became a unique town in the whole of the United States. A patent was issued for 53.58 acres to the mayor, Simeon C. Richardson, in trust for the use and benefit of the occupants of Greenhorn and to his successors. This Government order is said to be the only one of its kind, granting a direct patent to a municipality; in effect, making Greenhorn a little principality, a law unto itself.

February 21, 1903, with E. G. Stevenson as mayor.

There were many active mines in the area. Records show that 2,000 people received their mail at Greenhorn City; however, voting rolls reveal the population of the town was between 500 and 700. Recent newspaper stories, trying to give a little local color to the old community, say there were thirty-two saloons, but actual records list only five. There was plenty of action, though, when the 500 men on the day shift and 300 on the night shift in the surrounding mines came to town to be separated from their pokes.

The total take from the mines was large, and so was the payroll. Incidentally, there were no Chinese in Greenhorn.

As the town grew beyond its original fourteen-acre limit, an election was held and a measure approved by the voters in 1903 to incorporate a larger area. Today the city limits cover 53.58 acres.

The town had a jail but no church or

City of Greenhorn Townsite Patent issued in 1912 to Simeon C. Richardson, mayor of Greenhorn from the U.S. Government, signed by Wm. Howard Taft, President of the United States.

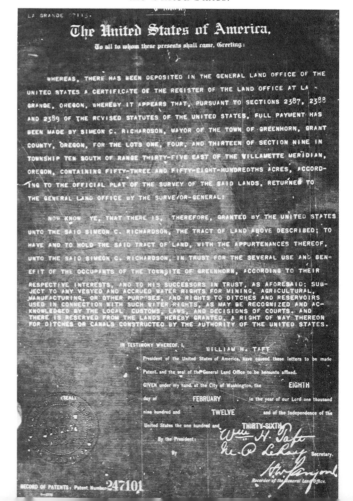

Leone Fleetwood photograph

Simeon Childs Richardson, the mayor of Greenhorn, was a good-looking gay blade in his day with his high plug hat, cut-away coat and gold cane. He married Leone Henley in 1898 and in 1901 came to Greenhorn. From that time on, he was the guiding light; a wise man with tremendous energy and drive. It was through his efforts that title was secured to the land of Greenhorn. He was active in incorporating the town and for development of the city water system. Richardson was a surveyor and helped to develop several mines in the area. He was known to all as Uncle Sim.

Leone Fleetwood photograph

E. G. Stephenson, Postmaster at Greenhorn; also the first mayor of the city.

Boarding house at the Golden Gate mine

The old Pyx Mine buildings east of Greenhorn. In the early days, there was a post office at this mine.

Boiler and vanner room at the Golden Gate Mine

A McCord photograph

The Golden Gate Mill boiler and vanner room. This mine was purchased by the Daines Gold Mining Company and soon included the Belcher property. Owned by John W. Douce and now owned by his son.

Mr. and Mrs. Walter Krause and Mrs. William Steward at the Golden Gate Mine. Mr. Krause is using snow to make ice cream instead of ice.

A McCord photograph
The Golden Eagle Mine in the Greenhorn district, located
in Baker County, E ½ S.15T.10S.,R35E.

The Greenhorn jail sat on the southwest corner of the city;
that is, it did until some citizens of Canyon City got carried
away, and so did the jail by the same group. It's now at the
Canyon City museum. The man who built the jail was very
proud of his work, so he held a one-man celebration and
wound up to be the first to occupy his own hoose-gow.

school, although half a hundred youngsters
lived there. Oregon wouldn't allow a school
to be built near a saloon, so, in order to skirt
the law, Greenhorn's children were shifted
from one building to another. At one time
Mrs. Kate Mullen taught school in the lobby
of the Red Lion Hotel, which had a saloon in
the back. It became a regular nutshell game
of "now you see it, now you don't."

Greenhorn was a boardwalk town, with
all the businesses crowded along Main
Street. Most of the buildings had the high
false fronts typical of early mining towns.
The homes were a mixture of log cabins and
frame structures. Light came from coal oil
lamps, and the plumbing was outside, with
a Sears, Roebuck catalog hanging on a con-

The Royal White Mine is one of the few gold mines in the
Greenhorn Mountains in operation today. It is located
about 2 miles N.E. of Greenhorn and is owned by the Ray
Myers family in Baker, Oregon.

venient nail. A few of the old buildings remain standing today.

Greenhorn's first water system — a well
and pumping plant — soon became inade-
quate. Through Richardson's efforts, the
state granted a water right to a spring high
on the mountain, and nearly a mile of five-
inch pipe was installed. This system remained in use until the early 1970s, when a
new plastic pipe was installed.

Two mail stages a day operated on a regular schedule. Deep winter snows hampered
traffic. When the stages couldn't get
through, the mail carrier let the horses pull
him on skis. A rope around his waist was
tied to the harness, and the mail sacks hung
from the hames. Skis and snowshoes were
not for pleasure in those days.

Greenhorn was a typical mining town,
and its story is the human story, with the
good and the bad of people who lived in
those high mountains. Among the prominent early citizens were Richardson,

Main Street in Greenhorn. There were no chair lifts in those days.

Main Street in Greenhorn City. The building at the far right is the famous old Red Lion Hotel. Jim Warren's saloon was in the back of the hotel. When the snow was deep, the stages let their passengers out on the upper deck of the porch. George Massamore's saloon was directly across the street and next to the flagpole.

Trouble on the main line when stage sled turned over

Mail carrier on skis, passenger on sled, horses pulling both. Note the mail sacks tied to the horses hames — tough going even when the mail got through.

Leone Fleetwood photograph
George Massamore, saloon keeper and stage driver between Greenhorn and Tipton.

Leone Fleetwood photograph

Greenhorn's meat market was on the south side of Main Street next door to the Red Lion Hotel and Saloon. Jefferson Wisdom drove a light spring wagon with a flyproof box on the back. Wisdom delivered meat to all the mines within driving distance. He served on the city council from July 15, 1907 to March 4, 1911. He also served as postmaster. Wisdom is the man with the white shirt and sleeveholders.

The old Carpenter cabin on the edge of the town of Greenhorn was built in the early 1860s and is still standing.

McWillis Gulch placer

Stevenson, and Miller; Sam R. Stott, city attorney; M. S. Jackson, editor of the *Greenhorn Investigator;* William H. Kelley, mine owner; William F. Draper, store owner; Jefferson D. Wisdom, owner of a meat market; Maude T. Draper and Alice Wiegand, who both served as post-mistresses; J. E. Millard and Jim Warren, saloonkeepers; William Peart, hotel proprietor; Bert Rogers, drugstore proprietor; Mr. and Mrs. Vic Mullen, hotel operators; and Ira Lemon, mine operator.

Others who helped guide the town through its early days were Mrs. Maggie Hardy, proprietor of the Greenhorn Restaurant; G. H. Wilson, mine owner and city recorder; George W. Massamore, saloon-keeper and mail carrier; George R. Wiegand, city treasurer; Dorfman and Rosenthal, general mercantile store operators; Mr. Rosenbaum, who ran the Alexander Clothing Company; M. Holden,

an assayer; and Andy Larsen, a well-known pocket hunter.

When the mines closed down so did the towns, which had sprung up like mush-rooms throughout the gold belt. Some lingered on for a number of years, but one by one they became ghost towns. Greenhorn lasted until December 15, 1919 when the post office closed. Sagebrush crept back into the streets, wind whistled through broken windows, and pack rats set up shop in once-busy stores. Then came a fire that wiped out many of the buildings.

Not long ago a small boy from Idaho stood reading the Forest Service marker. When he came to the part which says, "Two thousand people lived here," he looked at the five or six remaining buildings and said to his mother, "If that's all the houses they had, they must have had awful big families in those days."

WHEN THE MINERS DANCED

THE FIDDLE AND THE ORGAN FURNISHED the music; people flocked from all over the mountain to attend the Saturday night dances. They came on foot, on horseback, in buckboards and light spring wagons filled with straw, until the hitching rails and livery stables were filled.

The dance hall had a platform stage at the back and a large wood stove in one corner. Coal oil lamps were set in wall brackets. The women sat on rough benches along the wall, while the men stood together near the door. On the stage sat the fiddler and the organ player. After a few delays the fiddler tucked his instrument under his chin, took a few trial runs with his bow, and they were ready.

The square-dance caller came forward: "Grab your partner and don't be late, swing your partner like swingin' on a gate." And the dancers were off, stomping and whirling.

What the music lacked in quality was made up in quantity — each beat was punctuated by the stomp of the fiddler's feet. Equidistant between the musicians stood a brass spittoon, and both men qualified as expert marksmen. When the kids got sleepy they were bedded down around the stove. The dancing continued until daylight, the only intermission being for a midnight supper or an occasional fist fight.

As the evening drew along, the tempo changed from *Money Musk* and *Little Brown Jug* to dreamier waltzes. At last came the old familiar *Goodnight Ladies*, the fiddler put down his bow, and the dance was over.

The kids were counted and stowed in the wagons, while Mom and Pop sat on the front seat. Now and then Mom sat alone, stiff as a ramrod, with Pop poured into the back with the kids. Pop was stiff, too, but not for the same reason. There were few sources of amusement in the early days, and square dances were a rare chance to blow off steam.

The Red Lion was one of many frontier hotels — warm and comfortable but short on luxury. It stood at the east end of Greenhorn, on the south side of Main Street, and was operated by Mr. and Mrs. Bill Mullen. In the rear, separated from the lobby by swinging doors, was a saloon run by Jim Warren.

Along one wall of the hotel lobby were rows of potted geraniums in five-pound lard pails. A large wood heater stood in the center of the room. On one wall hung a calendar put out by a harness maker. A few stiff-backed chairs, a rocker or two, and a sofa against the wall completed the decor.

The bedrooms upstairs were furnished with brass bedsteads, a commode with china washbowl and pitcher, a chair beside the bed, and a coal oil lamp in a wall bracket. On the back porch was a wooden trough with wash basin, soap, a roller towel, and a comb attached to the wall by a chain. No need to ask whether there was a crowd in town; the roller towel gave you your answer.

Jim Warren's Red Lion Saloon. Note the swinging doors leading into the lobby of the Red Lion Hotel. The men in the picture from left to right are August Hornicker; Mr. Fredrick, caretaker at the Liston Mine; Jack Dockery; J. W. Clark; E. G. Stevenson, the first mayor of Greenhorn and later postmaster; Marcus Henley, Mrs. Richardson's son; Andy Larsen, a pocket hunter; Ed Bartlett, the bartender; and city marshal, Jack Marshall.

Jim Warren worked hard at keeping his saloon respectable. Every town had its saloon moochers, and in Greenhorn there was Old Pete. He was well lubricated one night in Warren's saloon, so the bartender, Jack Marshall, offered him a pint of whiskey if he would get lost for the rest of the evening. Old Pete was agreeable. Placing the pint in his hip pocket, he started on unsteady legs through the swinging doors. Just at that moment a husky miner burst in from the lobby and bumped into Old Pete, knocking him flat on his back on the floor. There was the sound of breaking glass. After a while the old fellow felt his wet leg. "Are you hurt, Pete?" asked the bartender. The old-timer answered, "By God, I hope so."

Each mining camp was a world unto itself. The long winter months seemed to draw people together. To the children, the

Large granite rock on Main Street in Greenhorn. Note holes drilled in the top; this is where the rock drilling contests were held.

community Christmas tree was the high-light of the year.

The tree stood on the stage of the dance hall, almost touching the ceiling. The ladies popped corn and strung it to decorate the branches. A homemade tinsel star twinkled from the very top, while colored candles shone from the boughs. Rich and poor were there, and for that evening they were all equal. Every child received a present. Bags of candy and nuts, popcorn, even popcorn balls were passed out. A crate of oranges came all the way from Baker City by stage, and each youngster received an orange. If you've never been a child in an early-day mining camp, you don't know the value of an orange.

Folks sat on benches facing the stage as the program got under way. One of the portly citizens of the village was Santa Claus. The same organist who played for the dances now solemnly performed *Silent Night*. Christmas was one night when the bars and gaming tables stood empty.

One by one or in groups the children trailed up onto the stage to recite or sing. It was an evening anticipated by old and young alike, and never to be forgotten.

Rock-drilling contests were held in all mining camps on special holidays. The large, flat granite rock with the many holes drilled in it was known to the hard-rock miners as Contest Rock. Each Fourth of July and Labor Day they held contests to see who could drill a hole the fastest. All drilling was done with hand drills and heavy jackhammers.

A drilling team consisted of two men. One would strike for a minute at a stretch while the other turned the drill. The timekeeper ticked off the seconds as the water tender poured water into the hole alongside the drill. At the end of each minute the pair changed jobs without losing a stroke. The striker passed the eight-pound hammer to his partner with his free hand, while reach-ing for a longer drill and sticking it into the hole.

So it went for fifteen minutes, amid the echoes of steel on steel. The water mixed with the rock dust to form mud; each time the big hammer came down, the drill would bounce, splattering mud all over the toiling men. When the fifteen minutes were up, the keeper called time. Then the opposing team stepped up to the rock and drilled for another fifteen minutes. When the time was up the judges came forward, measured the holes, and declared the winners.

Bill Cola and Ira Lemon were the Green-horn champions for a number of years, while Al Gutridge and his partner held the Sumpter title. One Labor Day they met at Greenhorn. The betting was heavy, and when the contest was in full swing every business house in town was empty. So were the pockets of the Greenhorn sports when the contest was over!

The following year they met in Sumpter, and this time the Greenhorn boys carried away the loot. Their victory was of short duration. From one of the saloons stepped a brawny man named Dan Dunn. Before the Greenhorn boys could spend their money, he challenged the winning team. There is no record of who turned the drill for Dunn, but he and his partner raked in the chips, and the Greenhorn boys trailed back up the mountain — broke, as usual.

The Fourth of July celebration was a real jamboree in all mining towns. It started with a grand parade, followed by footraces, catching a greased pig, horse races, and prize fights. At night came the grand ball. Men were young and full of fun, and, as the night wore on, the "bottled brave maker" made would-be champions of them all.

Greenhorn had no regular doctor, so Bert Rogers served as doctor *pro tem*, and his drugstore was the cure-all center. Bert was affectionately called "Doc" by all. He knew how to administer Epsom Salts and tincture of iodine, and how to tell mothers the

The Diadem Mine in Grant County, on and one-half miles southwest of the town of Greenhorn.

The Bi Metallic mine, first known as the "Intrinsic" is located at the head of Salmon Creek in Grant County, N.E. ¼ Sec. 7, T 10 S., R 35 E., 2½ miles N.W. of Greenhorn; a gold and silver mine with 3,000 feet of tunnels. It was once owned by M. C. Carson of Boise, Idaho, the man standing in the picture.

A McCord photograph

The Psyche Mine is located three miles west of the town of Greenhorn at the head of Blue Gulch. A 24-stamp mill was placed in operation at one time.

The Big Johnny Mine is high on Vinegar Butte at the head of Blue Gulch. Wolverine Jack, the man standing in front of the cabin, was killed when a section of the tunnel caved in.

secrets of turpentine and lard. He could pull a tooth for horse or man. He knew how to isolate a child with measles, mumps, or chickenpox: he simply hung a bag of asafetida around the child's neck! He could set a bone as well as the next. He also sold wallpaper, paint, and window glass.

A few doors away stood Miller and Draper — "Dealers in General Merchan-dise and Miner Supplies. Our Slogan — We deliver to any part of the mountain where it's possible to drive a team." Their stock consisted of groceries, dry goods, clothing, valises, hardware, and crockery, along with all miner's supplies. Along one wall ran a counter, behind which were shelves stocked with bolts of calico, gingham, and outing flannel. The shoe department sold heavy work shoes and knee-high gum boots. Dress shoes had buttons and sharp-pointed toes. Center tables were piled high with work clothes — Levi's, shirts, underwear (long johns), socks, hats, suspenders, sleeve holders, and belts. Canned goods of all kinds filled shelves along the wall. On the counter stood a coffee grinder, a plug tobacco cutter, and a wheel of yellow cheese. A pickle barrel and an open hundred-pound sack of brown beans were near by and handy, for the mining district was called "the brown bean frontier." Slabs of bacon called sowbelly were piled high on a table. Rows of coal oil lamps and lanterns stood at the end of the center aisle, filled with shovels, axes, picks, and jackhammers. A wall rack held a few old-style black powder rifles; a revolver or two hung by their trigger guards on a nail. Contrary to Hollywood, the real sourdough scorned the use of a pistol to settle an argument. Two pick-hardened fists were good enough.

In the rear of the store stood a pot-bellied stove surrounded by a pipe railing which was a resting place for the customers' feet. Six or eight straight-backed chairs and a box full of sawdust completed the furnishings. The general store was the news and political center of the community, even more than the saloon, and night or day the chairs were usually occupied. Whittling was a popular pastime, and during the long winter months as the arguments waxed hotter the pile of shavings grew higher.

The Snow Creek Mine is located two miles southwest of the town of Greenhorn in S.16.T.10S.,R.35E at the head of Snow Creek in Baker County. A 10-stamp mill was in operation here.

QUEEN CITY OF THE MINES

WE HAVE FOLLOWED THE STAMPEDE to the goldfields in Canyon City and on into the Greenhorn Mountains. Now we return to Auburn, the newly established seat of Baker County, where gold was first discovered. The town was booming. Freight wagons and pack teams arrived daily from The Dalles and Umatilla Landing, and stages ran on a regular schedule of three trips a week each way.

A large part of the best placer mining ground in eastern Oregon was arid, and soon the Auburn mines and the town itself were faced with a serious situation. Water for mining must be found.

William H. Packwood took the lead, and in August 1862 the Auburn Water Company was organized. Without it, Auburn would have died.[59] A large reservoir was built on the hill above town, and a ditch four feet wide at the bottom was begun, tapping the waters of Salmon, Marble, Mill, and Pine creeks. Before it reached Auburn, the big ditch was sold to the Auburn Canal Company. Total construction cost was $225,000. This was the first of many large mining canals east of the Cascades.

Distributing ditches were extended to the mines. The cost to gold-seekers was high. To reduce the fee to twenty-five cents for a miner's inch of water, the white miners finally consented to allow Chinese to operate their own mines. This was the first breakthrough for the Orientals.

Within a year every inch of ground around Auburn was claimed. Still men arrived, eager to find their fortune. As word spread of new bonanzas, more seekers came. Each new strike established a new town. Westward came Sumpter, Bourne, Granite, Alamo, and Lawton; Winterville, Parkerville, Gimletville, and Geiser. All were booming mining camps — as long as the gold lasted.

In 1864 Colonel J. S. Ruckel realized the ore of the Virtue Mine in Baker County was fabulously rich. The trouble was, there was no water at the mine to run a quartz mill. He and the other owners of the mine decided to build the mill on the upper reaches of the Powder River, a few miles from the mine site. From this mill, another town was born. The town and the county were named for Colonel Edward Baker, a Civil War hero.

Nobody realized this little upstart village would become the financial center of a vast mining district, with bank deposits of over $1,500,000. The boom at Auburn was beginning to slow down, and many merchants and miners decided to cast their lot with the new town. Its location was more desirable, being closer to the Oregon Trail, which was used by both freight wagons and stages moving eastward into Idaho.[60]

The county seat was moved from Auburn to Baker City in 1866, and a post office was opened, with William McCrary as postmaster. He had been the first postmaster at Auburn. That same year a mail route was established between Baker City and Canyon

Courtesy Oregon Historical Society

Freighting supplies from Umatilla Landing to the mining towns in Baker area before the arrival of the railroad.

Baker, Oregon in 1866, the year the county seat of Baker County was moved from Auburn to Baker. Two years before, Colonel J. S. Ruckle, owner of the famous Virtue Mine, realizing he had a fabulously rich mine but no water, decided to build a water-powered quartz mill on the Powder River at the present site of Baker. The town of Baker City grew up around this mill.

A McCord photograph

The cabin at the 16-to-1 Mine near Olive Creek. Someone asked an old-timer how it received its name; he said, "Because the owners put $16 into the mine for every $1 they took out."

A McCord photograph
The McCord blacksmith shop and foundry was in the early days perhaps the most important business in the city as in all frontier towns. Wagons had to be repaired, horses shod, and mining equipment repaired. All night long one could hear the pounding of the hammers for freight wagons had to be conditioned for the long journey to Umatilla Landing for supplies.

City, linking the two great goldfields of eastern Oregon.

A. H. Brown opened the first store, located at what is now First and Valley Streets. The first saloon was on Front Street. Sam Rogers ran the first boardinghouse, while a Catholic priest named P. De Roo constructed the first hotel, the Arlington. Reynolds and Ferguson operated the express office, later run by the Wells Fargo Express Company.

The McCord Blacksmith Shop and Foundry was perhaps the most important business; as in all mining camps and frontier towns, wagons needed to be repaired. All during the night one could hear the pounding of the hammers as the wagons were conditioned for the long journey from the goldfields to the supply points at The Dalles and Umatilla Landing. They were not only blacksmiths; McCord's built wagons, stages, and sleds from the ground up. S. B. McCord also operated a hardware store and became Baker City's first official mayor. O. H. P. McCord, his son, was a leading citizen of Baker and a recognized historian of the early mining days. Many of his pictures appear in this book.

By 1870 Baker City had its first newspaper, the famous *Bedrock Democrat*. The Virtue Bank opened its doors in 1872 and purchased $200,000 in gold each year for the next ten years. All merchants were buyers of gold; they also took gold dust in exchange for merchandise, shipping it direct to their correspondents in Portland or San Francisco.

Baker City was incorporated in 1874; by 1879 the population was 1,193. Only 143 women and 166 Chinese were in the community. But by 1883 so many Orientals lived in Baker that a Chinese joss house was built.

In 1880 the county built a road to Canyon City in an effort to deflect some of the trade going over the old military road there to The Dalles. A network of stage lines ran in all directions from Baker City, connecting it with the mining districts. Later a stage line went from Baker City to the nearest railroad at Kelton, Nevada.

Baker was never just a mining town. It had a certain stability, as indicated by its schools and churches. Nevertheless, it was a colorful town, with all-night saloons, gambling houses, and hurdy-gurdy dance halls patronized by gamblers, miners, ranchers, cowboys, and sheepherders. A section of downtown was set aside as a red-light district.

This fine O. H. P. McCord display of gold will never be on display again for shortly after this picture was taken, the entire priceless treasure was stolen.

A McCord photograph

James F. Furguson, old-time cashier of the Virtue Bank in Baker, established in 1870. This bank purchased an average of $200,000 a year in raw gold for a number of years. Note the old-time typewriter. The bank burned in 1888.

The late O. H. P. McCord and his son, Robert, with parts of the gold display in their real estate and insurance office. Mr. McCord, Sr. was the son of S. B. McCord, the first mayor of Baker. He was a leading citizen of Baker and one of the few recognized historians of the early mining days. We are indebted to Mr. O. H. P. McCord and his family for many of the pictures in this book.

There was quite a contrast between the free-wheeling-and-dealing mining towns and those of the Willamette Valley, where the seat of state government was located. In May 1865 the state legislature passed the following law:

If any person shall keep open any store, shop, grocery, bowling alley, billiard room, tippling house or do any work other than for necessity or mercy on that day of the week commonly called Sunday, (he) shall be punished by a fine of not less than $5 or more than $50.

Perhaps this should not seem strange when we consider that this same state legislature, as late as 1905, passed a bill providing for a whipping post. The penalty was twenty lashes, and this bill was not repealed until six years later.

People in the mining camps paid little attention to this Puritanical thinking. They went right ahead digging gold at the rate of $3,000,000 annually. With a payroll of $750,000, things were booming.

The transcontinental railroad came to Baker City in 1884. This development brought in the Oregon Lumber Company, under the guidance of David Eccles. The company built a narrow-gauge railroad through the center of eastern Oregon's mining country. It was known as the Sumpter Valley Railway and cost $1,500,000. The two railroads funneled a great amount of business into the city.

By 1897 there was telephone service connecting Baker City, Canyon City, Sumpter, and all the large mines. By 1900, ten thousand people were living in Baker City.

The First National Bank of Baker City was incorporated in 1883; by 1897 it showed a cash balance of $710,344. The man instrumental in establishing the bank was Levi Ankeny, adopted son of Alexander P. Ankeny, a steamboat man from West Virginia. Levi also operated banks in Walla Walla and Pendleton.

Baker had twenty hotels, seven churches, two high schools, three public and one pri-

J. W. Wisdom drug store, corner Main and Valley Streets — 1885 — present location of J. C. Penney's.

Baker City soon became the supply center for all the mines in eastern Oregon and part of Idaho. First with pack trains and freight wagons and later two railroads. Stage lines using four to six horses operated out of Baker City. Working on a regular schedule to all the mining towns and camps in eastern Oregon. During the gold rush they were loaded with miners, promoters, gamblers, drummers, saloon keepers, Chinese, peace officers, army people, preachers, circuit judges and scarlet women. For many hours this cross-section of humanity sat side-by-side, a chummy little crowd, each absorbed in his or her own business.

Gay blades enjoying a glass of beer in the good old days

In the GOOD OLD DAYS
When Men were Men

A McCord photograph

A friendly poker game in Baker. The old colored man is
Oscar Johnson, the bartender. Members of his race were
rare in the early-day mining towns.

Baker City, Oregon in 1880. Baker had 1,197 inhabitants.
There were only 143 females living there and some of
those were carrying on a business as old as the hills. They
were restricted to what is known as Resort Street. One
hundred sixty-six Chinese lived in Baker at that date.

The famous old hotel Warshauer, later sold to Albert Geiser, owner of the Bonanza Mine, and renamed the
Geiser Grand. This three-story brick hotel was considered the finest hotel east of The Dalles. It even had an
elevator. The dining room had a seating capacity of 200. Just off the lobby was one of the most luxurious bars
in the state. The hotel had electric lights, hot and cold water, and bathrooms, but the lavatories were at that
early date all on the main floor.

Courtesy Oregon Historical Society

This picture of Baker was taken on February 1, 1911 when the name was changed from Baker City to just plain Baker. The present population is close to 10,000. Baker is located in almost the exact geographical center of eastern Oregon's gold fields. Today it is a clean modern city with a glorious past.

vate school, a city-owned water system, six general stores, three department stores, and two hardware and implement stores. Among the hotels was the famous Geiser Grand, one of the finest in the West, with seventy steam-heated rooms and a hydraulic elevator. Other well-known hotels were the Sagamore, the Antlers, and the St. Lawrence. There were many restaurants, two daily newspapers and one weekly, fifteen saloons, a modern hospital, and a city-owned horse-drawn streetcar line. Henry Rust, who claimed he hadn't taken a drink of water in thirty years, operated the brewery. He also ran the opera house next door.

The Grier and Kellogg livery stable and

The P. Basche store was established in 1865. During the early mining days this company sold most of the heavy equipment used in the surrounding mines, such as pumps, hydraulic giants and stamp mills.

Rust's hall and brewery in Baker. Mr. Rust boasted that he had not tasted water in 30 years. Rust's hall was the principal amusement resort. It seated 800 people. When a good road show was in town, the hall was full. Dances were also held in the hall. There was a bar in the front of the building and there were many fights. A man named McCarty hit a man over the head with a beer bottle and killed him. In 1897 fire destroyed the building. Rust served on the council and was once mayor of Baker.

stage office was on the corner of Main and Auburn, where the Baker Hotel stands today. Established in 1865, the stage line covered the entire mining area of eastern Oregon.

In 1911 "City" was dropped, and the name became just plain Baker. Oregon has many modern towns, but few can boast such a glorious past.

The Grier and Kellogg livery stable and stage office was on the corner of Main and Auburn where the Baker Hotel stands today. All of eastern Oregon and all mining camps were served by this company starting in 1865. They were also agents for the Wells Fargo Express. Millions in raw gold were transported by this company.

The large building on the left with the clock is the "Geiser Grand" Hotel. Note the street car tracks.

THE VIRTUE DIGGINGS

THE CITY OF BAKER OWES ITS BEGINNING to the mines in the Virtue district, about ten miles east of town. Most of the gold came from the Virtue Mine, discovered by a miner on his way to Idaho. He sold the prospect to Colonel J. S. Ruckel, who worked and developed the mine for four years. It was then sold to J. W. Virtue and A. H. Brown and was named the Virtue Mine.

The ore at the mine was known as free-milling, and the prospect became the first large-scale quartz mine in eastern Oregon. It is believed to have produced $2,200,000 from 1862 to 1924.[61] It was among the first mines with a modern twenty-stamp mill and hoisting house. One sample on display at the Virtue Bank in Baker is the size of a hen's egg and contains $400 in gold. Samples from the Virtue Mine on display in 1898 ran $100,000 to $200,000 per ton. Five hundred dollars was pounded from a five-pound chunk with mortar and pestle.

The First National Bank in Baker exhibited a ten-pound chunk of white quartz from the same district that ran $275,000 per ton and a saucerful of quartz samples from the Auburn district valued at $4,000,000 per ton — it was three-quarters pure gold![62]

Virtue later sold his holdings to San Francisco interests. Other mines in this group were the Flagstaff, Emma, Hidden Treasure, Friday, Rachel, Mable, and White Swan. Before the days of hard-rock mining, rich placers were found in the area between the Virtue and the White Swan.

The Flagstaff Mine, four miles north of the Virtue, was discovered in 1894. Franklin Mallory of Spokane bought a one-third interest for $20; within six months the mine was sold to French interests for $20,000, and production later reached $100,000 a year. The White Swan, three miles southeast of the Virtue, was a heavy producer in the early days; production has been estimated at $724,000.[62] Records on other mines in the district are scarce, but none is believed to have produced more than $200,000.[74]

New mines were discovered northeast of Baker City at Sparta, Sanger, and Cornucopia, also along the tributaries of the Snake River at Connor Creek, Weatherby, and Chicken Creek. In the early 1860s placer mining was carried on at Clark's Creek, a few miles south of what is now Bridgeport, in Baker County. The camp became known as Clarksville. From 1917 to 1936 a small dredge worked on the lower reaches of Clark's Creek, and considerable gold was recovered.

In 1868 a toll road was completed between Baker City and Bridgeport. The Clarksville post office moved to Bridgeport in 1876; Jere Dooley was postmaster at both places. Stice's Gulch, Rye Valley, Mormon Basin, and Malheur City were all in an area of heavy production of placer gold. Malheur City was in important mining town as early as 1863. Gold was plentiful, but not water. The famous Eldorado Ditch later supplied water to Malheur City, Eldorado, and

The gold exhibit at the United States National Bank in Baker, Oregon is one of the finest to be found in the country. Most of the specimens have been found since 1897. The cream of the nugget crop went to the melting furnaces long years before specimen nuggets were held in esteem as collector's items. In the early days the melting pot was more important than an exhibit in a showcase.

The Virtue Mine eight miles east of Baker. According to Waldemar Lindgren, nationally known geologist, the production record of this mine up to 1902 was $2,189,000. Samples in the ticket office of the O.R.N. Company; in 1898 ran $100,000 to $200,000 per ton.

The gold scales on display in the U.S. National Bank in Baker. Over the years millions of dollars in raw gold was weighed on these scales before it started on its long journey to the mint in San Francisco.

Amelia. Malheur City was a ghost town for many years, but in 1957 it was destroyed by fire and the old cemetery is the only remaining landmark today.

Gold was discovered in southern Idaho and on March 3, 1863, Idaho became a territory. Stages, freight wagons, and pack trains moved day and night through Baker City from Umatilla Landing, going southeast to the mines in Oregon and southern Idaho. They traveled on toll roads and toll bridges owned by the Burnt River Bridge and Ferry Company. The toll receipts ran as high as $1,000 a day.[63] The stages used armed guards riding shotgun, while the men driving freight wagons and pack trains were armed with rifles. By 1863 Ben Holladay was operating daily stages from The Dalles and Umatilla Landing to Salt Lake City, and by 1870 the Pioneer Stage Line advertised it had reduced the time to three days from Umatilla Landing to Boise. Later these same stages met the railroad in Utah as the tracks continued moving westward.

The White Swan Mine in the Virtue district about 10 miles east of Baker is reported to have produced $700,000. Gold was discovered in the district in 1862.

The White Swan Band. The White Swan Mine changed hands several times and while it was a good mine, it fell into the hands of promoters more interested in selling stock than in mining. In 1901, the manager of the mine presented the Baker City Cornet Band with new uniforms and the band's name was changed to The White Swan Band. In 1907, he gave them what was then the largest bass drum in the world, six feet in diameter. The band was used in the promotion of the sale of mining stocks. The U.S. Government put a stop to it, and the name was changed to the Baker Concert Band. For years Louis E. Fretag, known as Oregon's Little Sousa, was conductor. There was no reflection on the members of this fine band, one of the finest in the nation at that time.

Malheur City, originally in Baker County but now in Malheur County, is located on Willow Creek. Gold was discovered here in 1863. There was not enough water for placer mining until the Eldorado Ditch was completed in 1878. The ditch was 134 miles long, costing about $500,000. It was engineered by W. H. Packwood. *The Oregonian* stated Packwood for a short time realized $600 every 24 hours. Mining in the area slowed down and the ditch never paid for itself. Malheur City was destroyed by fire August 16, 1957. The old cemetery is still cared for by the descendents of the old-time residents of the town.

The Blue Bird Mine was in the Alamo and Lawton district near the Red Boy Mine

BONANZAS BY THE DOZEN

MANY INTERESTING TOWNS SPRANG UP OVERNIGHT. Sparta is one of them. If you believe in ghosts, you should find a few here. Sparta was first known as Kooster, named after a Dutchman who struck pay dirt at the head of Maiden Gulch. Until 1870 Gemtown, a mile west, was a successful rival, but Gemtown faded away and Kooster became Sparta, named after William Packwood's hometown in Illinois.

The Leiken brothers were among the first arrivals; they owned one of the richest claims, known as Old Dry. This was a surface mine worked with an old-time rocker; the ore was hauled to water by oxen. Even so, the brothers cleaned up $30,000 in two years.[64] The Harkerader brothers were owners of another good pocket, so rich the first pan of dirt produced $50 in gold. They took $10,000 from a piece of ground sixty by two hundred feet. On one trip E. E. Clough and his father hauled $25,000 in gold dust to Baker City in their wagon.[64]

The ground was rich with gold, but many of the original pioneers grew discouraged because there was no water to work the ore. Moneyed men became interested, and in 1870 William Packwood, Jim Virtue, and two or three others conceived the idea of building a ditch from Eagle Creek, about thirty-two miles away. Chinese pick-and-shovel labor dug the long ditch for twenty-five cents a day. It was completed in 1873 and furnished 3,000 miner's inches of water.

With plenty of water, the town of Sparta took on new life, growing quickly into a boomtown with a population of three thousand. The two largest general stores were owned by George Griggs and E. B. Cohn & Company. The town received its post office in 1872, with William W. Ross the first postmaster.[65]

Among the richest placer claims was the Shanghai-Moultrie, which produced an estimated $500,000. Others were the Maiden, Thorn, Blue, Murray, Rattlesnake, Sawmill, and Iron Gulch.

G. W. Estabrook, one-time postmaster, succeeded in inducing the merchants and some of the miners to send their gold dust through the registery department of the post office during the two years he was there. The two leading merchants averaged shipments of $15,000 a week. Three Chinese companies at Sparta shipped $4,000 a week to San Francisco during the same two-year period. Estabrook calculated that the total mail shipments reached $700,000 for the two-year period.[50] It has been estimated that the Sparta district produced $5,000,000.

All that remains of the historic town is the old general store built in 1873 by W. H. Heilner. However, people have found quartz seams and pieces of quartz float that were rich in ore. Perhaps someday someone will uncover the lode that poured $5,000,000 of coarse gold through the gulches surrounding Sparta.

The old mining camp of Sanger, in Baker

A McCord photograph

The Sparta Stage heading down to the famous Sparta Grade where hairpin curves bore such names as Dead Man's Curve. The stage is heading for Baker.

The Gem Mine is one of the very old mines in the Sparta district in Baker County, Sections 17 & 20, T.8S., R.44E. about 30 miles northeast of Baker, Oregon. Gold was first discovered in this area in 1863.

The Baisley-Elkhorn Mine crew. The estimated production was $950,000. The mine was discovered in 1882. It is located in Baker County, Secs. 20 to 21, T.8S, R.38E, near the head of Pine Creek about 15 miles from Baker; very poor road the last few miles.

County, was first called Hogum. This was later changed to Augusta and then to Sanger in honor of the owner of the Sanger Mine. Like other camps, Sanger was troubled by a shortage of water until a ditch was dug, bringing flow from Eagle Creek. Mining was placer at first; $500,000 came from this operation. Later there were several rich lodes, the Sanger Mine being one of the big producers. U.S. Mint reports show that from 1889 to 1890 production was $813,000; estimated total production was $1,500,000.[66]

Courtesy Oregon Historical Society

The white miners as a rule were cruel to the Chinese. The store keeper at the mining town of Sparta said, "The Chinese purchased rice and gum boots while the whites bought whiskey." In Jacksonville a drunk shot and killed a Chinaman. The white was fined $25 for shooting a gun in the city limits.

A McCord photograph

One of the first water-powered Arrastras; located at the Sanger Mine was used for grinding ore

A 10-stamp mill in operation at the Sanger mine near Baker about 1890. Stamps were mechanical crushers used to pulverize the quartz rock to free the gold. Mercury was then used to pick up the gold.

Courtesy Oregon State Department of Geology and Mineral Industries

Sanger was located just below the Sanger Mine near the road between Medical Springs and Halfway. It was the first known as Hogum. In 1871, the name was changed to Augusta in honor of Augusta Packwood, the first unmarried woman to arrive there. Later the name changed again, this time to Sanger, the name of the principal mine owner. Sanger received a post office on August 17, 1887.

The Sanger Mine was discovered in 1870. It produced $1,500,000. It was located in the Eagle Creek district of Baker County, SW ¼ S.2, T.7S., R.43E.

Members of the Pete Mann Ditch Company that purchased the old-time mining ditch that wound around Greenhorn Mountain for 30 miles. This group was both miners and farmers. The miners using the spring run-off water and the Burnt River farmers using it the balance of the year for irrigation.

As has already been pointed out, much of eastern Oregon's best gold-bearing land was arid, and water had to be brought in for placer mining. The Auburn Ditch was completed first, followed by the ditch to Rye Valley. In 1873 the 32-mile canal was completed to the Sparta district. This was followed by the Sanger Ditch, and then came the Pete Mann Ditch in the Greenhorn Mountains, bringing water to the area around Robinsonville and Greenhorn. This ditch is still in use today, the water being shared by the Parkerville placers and farmers in the valley below.

Grandaddy of them all was the Eldorado Ditch in Baker County, largest of its kind on the Pacific Coast. It was five feet wide at the bottom, seven at the top, and 130 miles long. It carried water from the Burnt River to mines around Eldorado and Malheur City. Completed in 1873, the canal was so large it was used to float logs and building material to the mining camp. It, too, was built by Chinese labor.

Before these canals were completed — before the days of placer mining — gold was found chiefly in mountain streams, washed down from its source. Many fine specimens had gathered in depressions in stream beds. It was virgin ground, ideal for the early-day

Each nugget in this pan would make a beautiful piece of jewelry, but to the miner in the early days, it was just gold worth so much an ounce and another grubstake. (Dish U.S. National Bank)

miner to work, as his tools were only a pick, shovel, gold pan, or sluice box.

Perhaps the most famous nugget was taken in 1873 from the McDonald and Caldwell claim on Gimlet Creek near the town of Whitney, about halfway between Sumpter and the Bonanza Mine. When gold was going for $20.60 an ounce, this nugget had a value of $17,000.

Gimlet Creek produced a number of fine nuggets. D. H. Stearns tells of specimens valued at $300, $800, $1,500, and $2,100, all taken from the same place on the creek. Stearns reports a kidney-shaped nugget valued at $3,200 found in 1870 by S. A. Caldwell. It was purchased by J. W. Virtue, who later sold it to Captain J. C. Ainsworth.[67]

Another nugget, valued at $14,000, was discovered in McNamee Gulch just a few miles south of Greenhorn City.[68] One valued at $3,000 was taken near the Bonanza Mine on a branch of the Burnt River. Postmaster Daggett of Robinsonville found one valued at $1,100.[69]

The Susanville district on the Middle Fork of the John Day River produced many fine specimens, including the famous Armstrong nugget now shown at the U.S. National Bank of Oregon in Baker. This weighs seven pounds and was valued at $2,500. Other nuggets from the same area were valued at $800, $625, and $480. Snow Creek, near Greenhorn, produced one valued at $600; Dixie Creek in Rye Valley yielded another at $640.

Connor Creek was known for its fine specimens of coarse gold. The total production from both placer and quartz mining is estimated at $1,250,000.[70] The Connor Creek quartz mine was among the heavy producers. A twenty-stamp mill crushed the ore for a number of years. In this mine were blocks of ore so hard they were piled to one side. Through curiosity one block was broken and, as the miners said, "It was lousy with gold." Thirty thousand dollars was taken from four tons of the hard rock.*

---

*Author's Note: Keep in mind that gold at that time was valued at $20.67 per troy ounce, not the present value of upward to $100 per ounce.

The famous Armstrong nugget, weight 80.4 ounces, found on Buck Creek near Susanville. Valued at $2,500 by George Armstrong.

Gold nuggets containing appreciable amounts of vein quartz indicating they are from a rich lode or pocket located fairly close to the placer deposit where they were recovered.

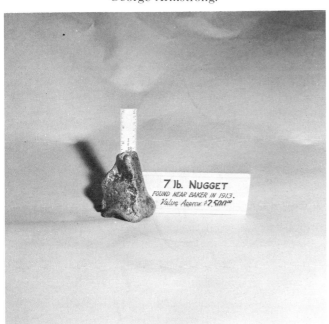

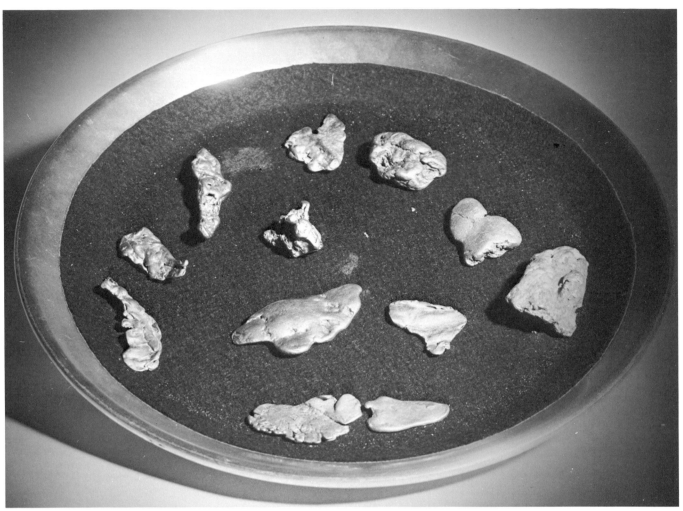

Gold nuggets polished and worn smooth by the action of water on bedrock

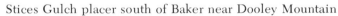

Stices Gulch placer south of Baker near Dooley Mountain

The Connor Creek lode mine is located three miles up Connor Creek from the Snake River. Some 8,000 feet of development work was done. The total output was about $1,250,000. Connor Creek was one of the first to be mined for placer gold in the early days. It has been estimated that over $2 million was taken from both lode and placer mining along the creek. Many fine specimens of gold nuggets came from Connor Creek. Probably the most placer gold was eroded from the Connor Creek vein.

Placer miners working in the Connor Creek district. Note the old half-barrel-type wheelbarrow.

The Nelson placers near Baker produced $400,000, much of it coarse gold. The Rye Valley placers produced more than $1,000,000. Work began there in 1862; some nuggets were reported to be as large as a hen's egg.

The Greenhorn placers were estimated to have produced $1,568,000.[71] Much coarse gold came from this area, which was considered pocket country. The *Sumpter Miner* on January 29, 1902 tells of the rich Worley Mine that joined the town of Greenhorn, with values running $1,100 per ton. A Portland newspaper said $500,000 was taken from the Worley. The ore was eighty per cent free milling.

Many more fine specimens were found, but we have noted only those that have been mentioned by historians over the years, the reason being that many an oldster was prone to stretch the truth a little. Some of these boys were prime candidates for the liars' club!

GOLDEN SUMPTER

GOLDEN SUMPTER, LOCATED TWENTY-NINE MILES WEST of Baker City, exploded into a boomtown when hard-rock mining came into its own. The rich ore attracted the attention of people around the world. Three South Carolinians settled near the present town in 1862. To express their pleasure at the fall of Fort Sumter in South Carolina during the Civil War, they named their primitive cabin Fort Sumter. Later the spelling was changed to Sumpter.

Joseph D. Young was the first postmaster, in 1874. For a number of years Sumpter remained a small town, its only connection with the outside world by wagon road over the hills from Baker City. This was the early-day stage route connecting all the towns and mines in the area. In placer days before hard-rock mining, the Downie, Dickson, and Ellis placers were the largest surface mines. Placer miners of the early sixties discovered most of the gold-bearing quartz ledges.

Sumpter started to grow about 1895, spurred by the advent of such modern equipment as the pneumatic drill, the stamp mill for crushing ore, and new chemical methods to extract gold from its alloys. The coming of the narrow-gauge Sumpter Valley Railway was an added stimulus.

The growth was rapid, from three hundred in 1897 to almost four thousand in 1903. Sumpter soon became known as the Queen City. There were three newspapers — one daily and two weekly. Seven daily stagecoach lines headquartered in Sump-

ter, serving the surrounding mining camps.

The railroad delivered as much as six carloads of mining machinery every day. It hauled six hundred carloads of timber a month to its mills in Sumpter and Baker City.[72] The tributary Sumpter payroll amounted to $2,000,000 paid to mining employees, the going wage being $4.00 for a twelve hour day.

On June 2, 1899, the *Sumpter News* checked the hotel registers. Among those listed were newcomers from Portland, Iowa, Spokane, Kansas City, Honolulu, Denver, Little Rock, Oklahoma, Michigan, Seattle, St. Paul, Pittsburgh, Sacramento, England, and Scotland. This was proof that Sumpter had a gold rush on its hands with people arriving from all over the world.

Starting in 1896, millions in gold flowed from the mines circling the Queen City. Another stream of gold came in from the mines for supplies. It was a booming town, and the sky was the limit, for news of the great gold strike carried round the world. The peak of the boom came in 1900, with an output of $8,943,486 from thirty-five mines.

Soon after modern methods made hard-rock mining profitable, a smelter was erected in Sumpter. It was a forty-ton plant, built in 1900. It was successful, but lack of operating capital forced a sheriff's sale. A second plant, called the Sumpter Smelter, was placed in operation in 1903. This was a one-stack smelter with a daily capacity of 100 tons. The mines hauling the most ore to the smelter were the Bonanza, Red Boy,

Sumpter, Oregon in 1895 just before the boom in hard rock mining.

Pack train carrying supplies to the mines

Sumpter was known as "Golden Sumpter," a gold mining town that grew in six years from a village of 300 to a boomtown of nearly 4,000.

It was on November 10, 1884 that the Oregon Short Line, a subsidiary of the Union Pacific, pushing northwest from Granger, Wyoming met the Oregon Railroad and Navigation Company's line coming in from the southeast at Huntington, Oregon. Thus completing the transcontinental railroad from East to West and soon became known as the Union Pacific.

Ben Harrison, Golconda, and Magnolia. For some unknown reason, most of the mines continued to ship their ore to the smelter at Tacoma, although the charges by rail were seven dollars a ton. Without the cooperation of the mine owners, the smelter was not profitable, so in 1907 it closed down. All that remain are the old foundation and the slag piles — a monument to the failure of smelting in the eastern Oregon goldfields.

In the 1899 and 1900 two Sumpter newspapers, the *Blue Mountain American* and the *Sumpter News*, mentioned the following among the business houses in Sumpter: seven hotels, five rooming houses, six restaurants, sixteen saloons, three livery stables, three blacksmith shops, one wagonmaker, seven general stores, three newspapers, two drugstores, five cigar stores, one cigar factory, three meat markets, two churches, one brewery, two banks, five

assay houses, one express office, four barbershops, two plumbing stores, six law offices, one opera house, one dance hall, one sawmill, three hardware stores, a volunteer fire department, telephone and telegraph offices, and an electric light system.

Also included in the establishments were a public school with four teachers and two hundred pupils, two galleries (one photograph and one shooting), one undertaker and, last but not least, a section of the city set aside as a red-light district. Later the city boasted a new hospital, a three-story brick hotel, and a third bank.

Sumpter must have been somewhat sophisticated for a mining town. On September 3, 1899, the *Blue Mountain American* announced the opera house was featuring *Snow White and the Seven Dwarfs*. Down the street a swanky joint called the Gem Saloon featured a lady orchestra. On Saturday nights the saloons were crowded

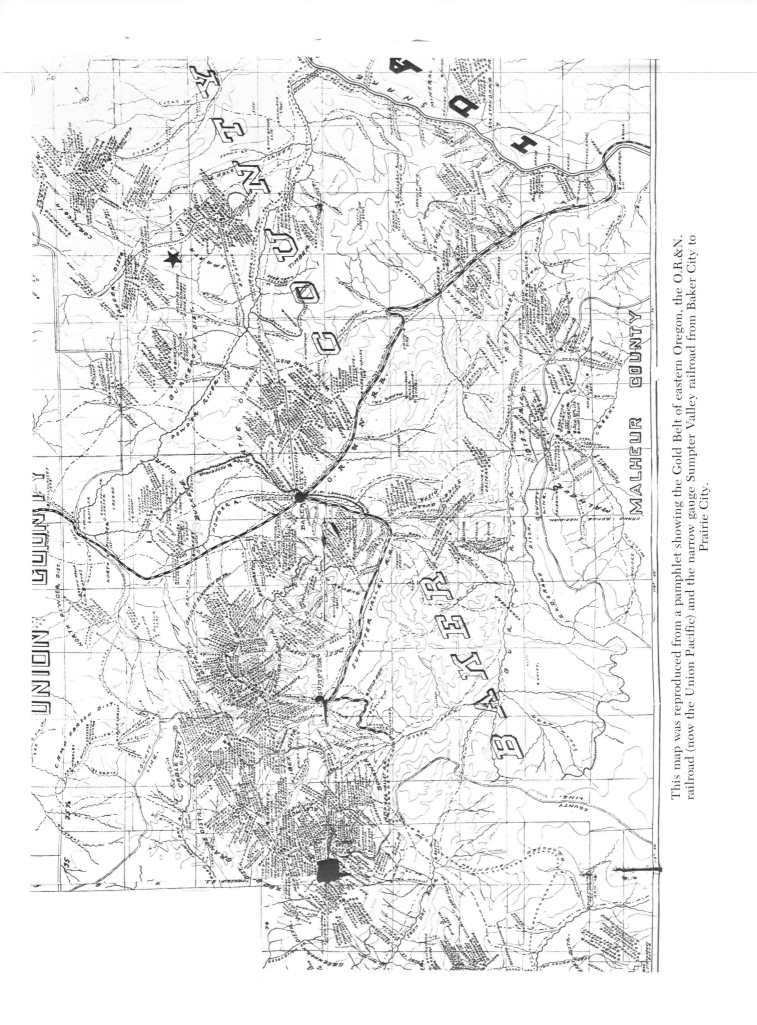

This map was reproduced from a pamphlet showing the Gold Belt of eastern Oregon, the O.R.&N. railroad (now the Union Pacific) and the narrow gauge Sumpter Valley railroad from Baker City to Prairie City.

The Oregon Smelting and Refining Company plant at Sumpter during the early 1900s.

Engine room at the Oregon Smelting and Refining Company.

A picture of the Sumpter Smelter crew at the time the smelter was running full blast.

with gamblers, dance hall girls, and miners whooping it up. Now and then a masquerade ball was held at McEwen's Dance Hall. Everyone, both rich and poor, attended, while the orchestra poured out the gay tunes of the day.

They held real celebrations in those days. In 1900 the Sumpter papers printed the official Fourth of July program:

The Grand Parade starts promptly at 10:00 A.M.
100-yard foot race, first prize $10.00
Boys handicap, 50 yards, $2.50
Girls handicap, 50 yards, $2.50
Three-legged, 50 yards, first prize $5.00
Tug-of-War, first prize $10.00
Greased pig, first prize winner keeps pig
Horse racing, first prize $100
Champion wrestling match, winner $50
Miners Hard-Rock Drilling Contest, Doubles
    winners $250 – Singles winner $75
Balloon ascension in public square at 6:00 P.M.
Grand Ball at Opera House

As in all early-day mining camps, the cost of living was high until transportation became better and homesteaders started to raise more than the miners could consume. Then prices began to tumble. Here are a few of the low prices: Eight pounds of coffee for $1.00; spring lamb at 10 cents a pound and mutton at seven cents; apples

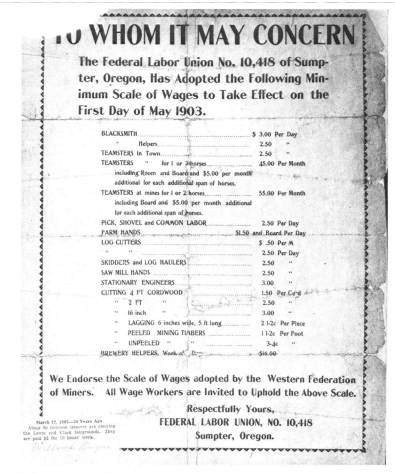

TO WHOM IT MAY CONCERN

The Federal Labor Union No. 10,418 of Sumpter, Oregon, Has Adopted the Following Minimum Scale of Wages to Take Effect on the First Day of May 1903.

BLACKSMITH	$ 3.00 Per Day
" Helpers	2.50 "
TEAMSTERS in Town	2.50 "
TEAMSTERS " for 1 or 2 horses	45.00 Per Month
including Room and Board and $5.00 per month	
additional for each additional span of horses.	
TEAMSTERS at mines for 1 or 2 horses	55.00 Per Month
including Board and $5.00 per month additional	
for each additional span of horses.	
PICK, SHOVEL and COMMON LABOR	2.50 Per Day
FARM HANDS	$1.50 and Board Per Day
LOG CUTTERS	$ .50 Per M
" "	2.50 Per Day
SKIDDERS and LOG HAULERS	2.50 "
SAW MILL HANDS	2.50 "
STATIONARY ENGINEERS	3.00 "
CUTTING 4 FT CORDWOOD	1.50 Per Cord
" 2 FT "	2.50 "
" 16 inch "	3.00 "
" LAGGING 6 inches wide, 5 ft long	2 1-2c Per Piece
" PEELED MINING TIMBERS	1 1-2c Per Foot
" UNPEELED " "	3-4c "
BREWERY HELPERS, Week of " D	$16.00

We Endorse the Scale of Wages adopted by the Western Federation of Miners. All Wage Workers are Invited to Uphold the Above Scale.

Respectfully Yours,
FEDERAL LABOR UNION, NO. 10,418
Sumpter, Oregon.

March 12, 1903—50 Years Ago
About 50 common laborers are clearing the Lewis and Clark fairgrounds. They are paid $2 for 10 hours' work.
Portland, Oregon

Labor Day was first celebrated in 1882, but was not recognized in Oregon until 1887. A shift in the mines was 10 hours and 12 hours in the mill, and both worked seven days a week. In May 1903, the Federal Labor Union No. 10,418 at Sumpter, Oregon adopted the above scale of wages.

The Midway Mine in the Sumpter area

C. W. Comdon photograph

The Sumpter Market; an idea of the way business was
conducted in a booming mining town.

$1.00 a box; flour $3.50 a barrel; potatoes $1.00 a sack, and onions 50 cents a sack. The Sumpter Bakery advertised two loaves of bread for five cents. The Griffin Hotel charged 25 cents for a meal and 25 cents for a room. The Eureka Chop House served all you could eat for 25 cents. All this when wages were $3.00 or $4.00 for a 12-hour day.

While Sumpter was a hard-rock mining town and its growth caused by rich underground veins, some placer mining claims were almost on the edge of town. The Downie placer, one and a half miles from Sumpter, produced $10,000 to $20,000 per year. Downie later leased the mine to the Chinese. The Ellis placers on Cracker Creek were also leased to Chinese, Ellis receiving royalties of $320 per week. The bank deposits were under so many names (a practice used by the wily Orientals) that it was impossible to check on production.

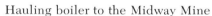
Hauling boiler to the Midway Mine

The Gem Saloon in Sumpter that featured a lady orchestra

The Bank of Sumpter about 1898

Grandstand and ladies' choir during the Fourth of July celebration in Sumpter

Fourth of July celebration in Sumpter

Hauling heavy mining machinery in the winter to a mine near Sumpter

Hauling armatures to power plant at Olive Lake; weight 16,000 pounds, using 14 head of horses; picture taken on street in Sumpter.

The Capitol, where the fire started that left Sumpter in ruins

The Sumpter Valley dredge boat started operation in Sumpter Valley about 1912. It is known as a bucketline dredge with a wooden hull upon which is mounted a continuous chain of buckets for excavating, a screening and washing plant, and a conveyor belt for stocking the tailings. Operation was discontinued in July 1954.

In 1902, a newspaperman wrote, "Sumpter, Golden Sumpter, what glorious future awaits thee?" The answer came on August 13, 1917 at 12:55 P.M. when 12 blocks in the very heart of the city were swiftly swept by fire with a loss of $500,000 — a mortal blow to Sumpter's dream.

About 1913 a new method of mining known as dredging started in Sumpter Valley, bringing a succession of both bucketline dredges and "doodlebug" washing plants. The first of the big bucket-line dredges was called the *City of Sumpter*. Its payroll constituted one of the mainstays to Sumpter's economy until it discontinued operations in 1954. The old dredge still stands at the edge of town.

Hard-rock mining started to slow down in 1907 but jogged along until the mortal blow came to Sumpter in the early morning of August 13, 1917. Fire broke out in the cook's room of the Capitol Hotel, and in three hours Sumpter was a pile of smoldering ashes. The loss was estimated at $500,000.

Yet the proud mining camp refused to die, and today it is a friendly town with a post office, school, stores, cafes, and shops. Among its citizens is A. H. Woodwell, a patriarch among assayers, a grand old man, and a symbol of the past. He has seen it all, and what stories he could tell!

Geologists say the great bulk of gold still lies hidden in the hills surrounding the former Queen City. Perhaps someday Golden Sumpter will rise again.

Harold McCall photograph

Close-up picture of the heavy steel dredge buckets capable of digging pay gravel 20 feet below the surface.

Harold McCall photograph

A "doodlebug" washing plant mounted on skids and operated on dry land; the ore fed by dragline or power shovel.

Mr. Woodwell, Sumpter's old-time assayer, a man with more knowledge of the surrounding mines than any living man, and a real gentleman at that.

This building during the early days was Sumpter's hospital. Today it is used by the Masonic Lodge.

All that remains of the two-story brick building that housed the Bank of Sumpter is the old vault with its steel door.

SITE OF BANK OF SUMPTER
SUMPTER, OREGON
BANK WAS ESTABLISHED IN 1899 WITH
A CAPITAL STOCK OF $10,000.00. THE
FIRST OFFICERS WERE A.P.GOSS,
PRESIDENT AND A.J.GOSS, CASHIER.
THE BANK WAS DESTROYED BY FIRE
ON AUGUST 13,1917 AND THE VAULT IS
ALL THAT REMAINS.

SUMPTER'S WONDERFUL NARROW-GAUGE

COMMONLY CALLED THE STUMP DODGER or the Mormon Special, the Sumpter Valley Railway was organized and incorporated in 1890 by David Eccles and a group of Utah stockholders. The same group organized the Oregon Lumber Company, constructing a sawmill on the outskirts of Baker City. Prime purpose of the railroad was to tap the vast timber resources of the area, but the road came at a time when hard-rock mining was in full swing. Eventually the railroad was completed through the very heart of the mining country for a distance of eighty miles.

The section from Baker to Sumpter was opened in 1897, as newspapers all over the world were attracting international capitalists to Sumpter and the surrounding mines. Experienced hard-rock miners, get-rich-quick camp followers, and business-men of all types flocked to the goldfields. Soon it became necessary to run four trains daily between Baker City and Sumpter. Large supplies of new mining equipment arrived every day. Heavy shipments of ore were hauled to the Sumpter smelter, and 800,000 pounds of concentrates were shipped each month by rail to the smelters in Tacoma and Everett, Washington.

The Oregon Lumber Company built its second large mill at Sumpter, and soon the railroad began climbing out of Sumpter Valley, bound for the timber on the headwaters of the Burnt River in the Greenhorn Mountains. The rails reached a new townsite called Whitney in June 1901.

Whitney is eleven miles southeast of Sumpter, at the junction of Camp Creek and Burnt River, in Baker County. The Oregon Lumber Company constructed its third large sawmill here. With the new mill in operation and ore shipments from the mines arriving every day, Whitney began its boom. A. W. King became the first mayor. The first school was taught by Lelia Thomas. Whitney received its post office in 1901; Austin Craig became the first post-master.

Whitney's newspaper stated that "you can judge the prosperity of a Western town by the kind and number of its saloons." Whitney had four, all doing a land-office business. The local trade was largely log-gers, miners, and stockmen; however, the trains and stages brought eastern capitalists seeking investments, promoters, drum-mers, merchants, saloon-keepers, gamblers, and a few females looking for an opportun-ity to shake some gold dust from the pockets of the miners.

The little town was proud of its two hotels — the Sumpter Valley operated by Mollie O'Farrel and the Whitney run by Mrs. J. A. Jollison. The two general stores carried everything from beans to blasting powder; one was operated by Miller and Draper, the other by Dorfman and Rosenthal. The Mint Saloon had a billiard and pool parlor. The Gem Saloon was owned by Riley Thomp-son, the Club Saloon by S. B. Saunders, and the Bonanza by Jim Warren and a man named Schepster. J. W. Copeland ran the

Sumpter Valley freight train, taken in Boulder Gorge in Powder River Canyon. Eight hundred thousand pounds of ore concentrates were shipped by rail from Sumpter to the smelters at Tacoma each month.

The Sumpter Valley Railroad hauled as high as 600 carloads of timber per month to the mills in Sumpter and Baker.

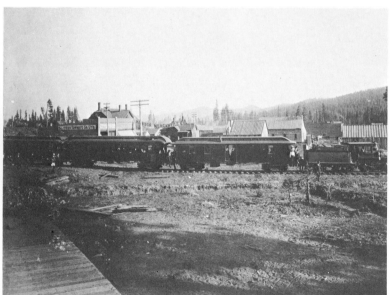

A McCord photograph

The narrow-gauge Sumpter Valley Railroad, commonly called the Stump Dodger, was built to tap the vast body of timber in Baker and Grant Counties. The line was completed from Baker to Sumpter in 1897 just at the beginning of the gold rush. Thousands of people were attracted to the area, and for a time it was necessary to run four passenger trains a day between the two towns.

Oregon Smelting and Refining Company in Sumpter, Oregon.

Courtesy Oregon Highway Department

This is all that is left of Whitney, once a busy little lumber and mining town on the narrow-gauge Sumpter Valley Railway, 11 miles southwest of Sumpter. It boasted a roundhouse and headquarters for stages heading for the mines in the area.

Whitney meat market, advertising "meat, poultry, fish, and game in season."

There were blacksmith shops owned by Jacobs and Hoffman. One advertised "We repair everything from a needle to an anchor." The other proclaimed that "we remove corns from horses feet 'free' to our customers." George C. Carter ran an assay office. John Totten operated the barbershop and charged twenty-five cents for a shave, haircut, or a hot bath in the back room. The Whitney Forwarding Company sold hay, grain, and flour. There were two newspapers and two livery stables.

Many miners wintered in Whitney. When the snow melted in the high mountains they were on their way again in the search for gold. Many carloads of ore were shipped to the smelter from this location. For a period of ten years it was a boomtown, but when the mines slowed down, so did Whitney. By 1910 the population had dropped to fifty-five people, and by 1950 it had reached zero.

Geiser was located eight miles west of

Whitney, along the road to Greenhorn. It was named for the family who for many years owned and operated the great Bonanza Mine. Geiser's sole purpose was to serve the people working in the mine, one

A McCord photograph

The wreck of a cattle train on the Sumpter Valley Railroad. The cattle scattered like quail in the timbered country. It took weeks to gather them again.

Part of the Oregon Lumber Company crew at Whitney in the early 1900s. Note the old-time cross-cut saws.

Sumpter Valley passenger train snowbound between Whitney and Austin; eight feet of snow fell on the mountain near Tipton.

of the largest in the state. It was not much of a town, but with the saloons, restaurants, and places of amusement, it kept the miners at home, to the delight of the mine owners.

However, the big story is not the town, but the Bonanza Mine. It was family-owned, no stock was ever issued, and it was fabulously rich — sort of a Cinderella story.

The mine was first located in 1877 by Jack Haggard. After two years he sold it for $350. It was never properly managed until 1890, when the Geiser family was forced to take it over to collect a $2,000 debt. Al Geiser, the older brother, turned out to be a mining genius. In nine years, the Bonanza Mine became one of the largest gold producers in Oregon, credited with having yielded $300,000 per annum. There are many tunnels and shafts, one to a depth of 1,200 feet. A 40-stamp mill was placed in operation. In 1899 the Geisers sold the mine to the Pittsburgh Mining Company for $500,000 in gold coin — a pretty good return on a $2,000 investment.

In 1904 the Sumpter Valley Railway extended its tracks to a new townsite called Tipton, six miles south of Greenhorn and ten miles by rail from Whitney. The town

Sumpter Valley passenger train entering Powder River Canyon.

Old Number 6 wood-burning engine was used for years on the run from Baker to Prairie City.

had a post office, hotel, and general store. Tipton was a little closer to the Greenhorn mines and soon became an important shipping point.

The railroad was again extended in 1908, this time to Austin in Grant County. Many mines as far away as Susanville were able to use Austin as a shipping point.

Located on the headwaters of the Middle Fork of the John Day River, Austin was a lumber town. It also served sheepmen, cattlemen, and miners. A man named Newton started the town. However, Minot Austin and his wife, Linda, arrived in 1888, purchased the townsite, and changed the name to Austin. Minot Austin ran a stage line between Sumpter and Canyon City, while

Left: Above — This is a picture of the town of Geiser, located at the Bonanza Mine. The town was company owned and boasted a post office, store, hotel, restaurant and also a saloon, butcher shop and a six-months school.

Left: Below — Two blacksmith shops worked ten days rigging wagons and shoeing horses to haul a huge boiler to the Bonanza Mine from Sumpter. They are using 18 head of horses. The horses hitched behind to a long pole, pushed.

Linda tended a general store, hotel, and boardinghouse. They say the old town once had a population close to five hundred. Mrs. Austin's store and boardinghouse did a flourishing business. It was headquarters for big sheep outfits that summered in the surrounding mountains. When the snow slowed down the mines, many a worker remembered the wonderful food put out by Linda Austin; with two saloons across the street it was a fine place to hole up for the winter.

The coming of the railroad boomed the town for a while, but it killed the cross-country stage lines, and the stages soon stopped operating. The Oregon Lumber Company started its own town named Bates about one mile down the river. A fine new mill was put into operation, and Austin slowly died.

My father summered sheep in the area, and when I was a boy of twelve I worked as a camp tender. I became sick with ptomaine poisoning on the trail and arrived at the Austin House in serious condition. Mrs. Austin put me to bed and nursed me like a mother. The saloonkeeper and our sheepherder recommended whiskey, but

The Bonanza Hoisting Plant

Miners and muckers at the Bonanza Mine, 1894. Note use of wax candles and "single jacks" — four pound hammers used with hand-held drill steel. Discovered in 1877 by Jack Haggard, the mine was sold for $350.

The Bonanza Mine is located eight miles west of Whitney on the road to Greenhorn

Vanner room at Bonanza Mine

C. W. Cowdon photograph

Austin was named for Mr. and Mrs. Minot Austin who came to the site in 1878. Minot Austin was the first postmaster. Mr. Austin's wife, Linda, operated a store, hotel and boarding house. Linda became famous for serving delicious food. Austin was both a railroad and stage stop.

The old pioneer stage lines carried passengers to every part of the west, but faster and more modern transportation such as the railroads and steam boats put them out of business. What tales these old wrecks could tell!

Courtesy Oregon Historical Society

Tipton, on the narrow-gauge railroad, was intended to be a lumber town and an ore shipping point for the mines in the Greenhorn Mountains. It was located six miles south of Greenhorn and 10 miles west of Whitney. It once boasted of having a post office, hotel and grocery store. The child in the picture is Nick Nokes, now editor of *The Oregonian*.

The Sumpter Valley passenger train on the run between Sumpter and Prairie City. The engine in this picture was affectionately known as Old Number 6.

Austin in 1908, the year the Sumpter Valley Railroad was extended from Tipton to Austin. The hotel and boarding house are at the right and on the left is the store and the saloon run by Jack Edwards.

Linda Austin would have none of it. One day while she was away they sneaked into my room with a tin cup of whiskey. When Mrs. Austin returned, she thought I was dead. I was dead all right — dead drunk! That was fifty-eight years ago, and I still don't know who to credit for my recovery.

In 1910 the railroad was extended once more, this time over Dixie Pass and down to Prairie City on the main John Day River. Very little ore was shipped over this section of the railroad, but it was popular for passengers and freight and for transporting livestock to market via Baker.

The decline of the Sumpter Valley Railway started in 1933 when the road was abandoned from Prairie City to Bates and Austin. All passenger service was suspended four years later, and the final scheduled run was in April 1947.

Old-timers loved to watch the wood-burning engines. Great piles of cordwood were stacked along the right-of-way and everyone pitched in at each stop to help load it. The grades were steep and it took a lot of wood to raise enough steam pressure. As a boy of twelve I rode the train from Austin to Whitney, and it was the thrill of my young life.

The roadbed was extremely rough, which was the reason old-timers named the train the Stump Dodger. Once there was a washout that demolished about a quarter mile of track. When it was repaired, the new roadbed was unusually smooth. They tell of the miner who was sleeping in the coach when the train reached the smooth spot. The old fellow jumped to his feet shouting, "Run for your life, boys, she's off the track."

CHAPTER SEVENTEEN

MOTHER LODE OF THE BLUES

BOURNE WAS STRICTLY A MINING TOWN, known all over the world for a brief period of time. Located on Cracker Creek, six miles north of Sumpter in Baker County, it was once called Cracker City. Jonathan Bourne, Jr., a Massachusetts lawyer, purchased the Eureka and Excelsior Mine (the E & E) in 1899; soon after, Cracker City changed its name to Bourne. Jonathan Bourne eventually moved to Portland and became a U.S. senator.

Gold was discovered on Cracker Creek in 1888 and the town came into being two years later. Bourne was surrounded by some of the best mining properties in eastern Oregon — the North Pole, E & E, Columbia, and others. These mines had a large payroll that contributed to the rapid growth of the town, which soon had a population of 1,500.

The Barings of London purchased the North Pole from Tom McEwen for $10,000, and soon the value of the property jumped to $2,000,000. The Barings were a wealthy English family. When they visited their Oregon mines they used the Hall Hotel in Bourne as headquarters. Before entering the dining room, Mr. Baring would order the room cleared, so he and his wife wouldn't be disturbed while being served.

Bourne became known as headquarters for all sorts of wildcat operators. Most famous among them was F. Wallace White, operator of the Sampson Company, Ltd. This company fleeced millions from people around the world. The promoters were too busy selling mining stocks to be interested in the orderly growth of Bourne. A plat was never made of the town, strung out along Cracker Creek Canyon. At one time 1,500 people received their mail at the Bourne post office. Later the town became incorporated and took on respectability, but, like the others, it gradually died away. By 1910 only seventy people were living there. A 1937 cloudburst washed away many of the buildings, and the 1950 census shows the town abandoned. The site has a few summer cabins and is surrounded by old mines and diggings, reminders of Bourne's glorious and not-so-glorious past.

Mines in the Cracker Creek district near Sumpter and Bourne tapped into what was known as the great mother lode of the Blue Mountains, reportedly one of the world's largest unbroken veins of gold. These mines furnished more than a quarter of the total of $17,000,000 for Oregon's gold output in the years 1896 to 1900. From 1900 to 1908, the Sumpter area produced $20,000,000 in gold; $12,000,000 of this came from fifty-three quartz mines.

The principal lode or quartz mines in the Cracker Creek district were the Columbia, E & E, Golconda, North Pole, Tabor Fraction, Bunker Hill, and Ibex. Of the group, the Columbia ran for the longest time. The Barings purchased the North Pole in 1895; the following year the mine produced $1,000,000. The E & E produced $1,000,000

The North Pole Mine was located in the 1870s. It is the Cracker Creek district between Sumpter and Bourne and has produced $2,485,006.96 since 1895.

The tramway from the North Pole Mine to the mill below.

The North Pole Mine lode is traceable for nearly five miles from Elkhorn Ridge southwesterly across Cracker Creek and Fruit Creek to McCully fork.

The Raymond Hotel in Bourne, Oregon; one of the two hotels. Today most of Bourne's business section is no more. Like most all mining towns, Bourne is just a memory of a wild and woolly era in our history.

The Columbia Mine starting in 1897 produced $3,638,959.60. It is located in the Cracker Creek district between Sumpter and Bourne.

Mammoth Mines and Mill near Sumpter, Oregon

A McCord photograph

Bourne, six miles north of Sumpter, was once known as Cracker City. It was surrounded by some of the best hard-rock mines in Oregon. The town once had a population of 1,500; 2 hotels, 4 saloons, 7 general stores, 2 newspapers, 3 restaurants, and 2 livery stables. One Saturday night the red light district burned, and while the crowd stood watching, the first man out of the burning building was the local preacher — where he went from there is not recorded.

in three years but was reported to have been poorly managed.

The Golconda was located in 1887 and sold for $24,000 the same year. Its gold was in rich chimneys, some of the ore running from $20,000 to $200,000 a ton. The Sumpter *Blue Mountain American* said in 1899 that the developers had uncovered a vein

where $50,000 was taken out in a few hours. The *Sumpter News* said in 1897 that one thirty-hour shift produced more than $10,000. The owners turned down an offer of $1,000,000 for the mine.

The Bunker Hill was reported to have produced $800,000 before being closed down. The Tabor Fraction reported a pro-

The Columbia Mine is located in the Cracker Creek district between Bourne and Sumpter T 8, R 37
E.W.M. Up to 1909, production was $2,553,031.31.

Cracker-Eagle Gold Mines on Cracker Creek near Sumpter

The Red Boy Mine is located on Congo Gulch, five miles southeast of Granite. It has been reported that the mine yielded over $1 million. There is about a mile of underground workings.

Assay office at the Red Boy Mine

An arrastra was a primitive device used to grind gold and silver ore. It was originally used by the Mexicans. The ore was spread on a floor, usually made of rock, and ground beneath heavy stones suspended from arms attached to a vertical shaft. At times horses were used to turn the shaft instead of a water wheel as shown here.

duction of $500,000 up to 1905, and the Baisly-Elkhorn, discovered in 1882, was reported to have produced $930,000 from 1905 to 1912.[72]

Twelve miles of tunnel ran through the mother lode on which most of these mines were located. Samples from three mines showed these values: Ibex, $29,500 per ton; Red Boy (near Granite), $30,000 per ton; and the Bonanza Mine in the Greenhorn Mountains, $20,000 per ton.

The Red Boy Mine was listed among the heavy producers, something over $1,000,000. Billy Graham, a storekeeper at Auburn, found the Red Boy in 1886 and sold his prospect to J. H. Robbins for $1,500. Later owners refused an offer of $2,500,000.

The first ore at Red Boy was crushed with an old-fashioned, water-powered arrastra.

Fourteen head of horses hauling heavy boiler on specially-made wagon to Red Boy Mine pictured on a street in Sumpter.

The Concord Mine belonged to the Red Boy group of mines.

The California Mine is in the Cable Cove district near the town of Bourne, Baker County, Secs. 14 and 15, T.85., R36E. discovered in 1873; mill erected in 1879.

In 1896 a modern 20-stamp mill was installed. The company worked forty-five men in three shifts for a number of years. Production during this time averaged $35,000 a month. The mine had 7,000 feet of tunnels, drifts, and crosscuts. The owners built a power plant on Congo Creek and a five-mile pipeline to the mine. (The plant also furnished electricity to the Ben Harrison, Bi-Metallic, Cougar, Independence, Buffalo, Monumental, Imperial, and California mines.) But hard times hit the Red Boy at last, and it was sold in 1916 at a sheriff's sale.

The Ben Harrison Mine, located high in the Greenhorn Mountains on Clear Creek, twenty-eight miles from Sumpter, was discovered in 1896 by Albert Gilliam. Much ore was shipped over the years to the Sump-

ter Smelter and later to Tacoma. It was complex ore and was never successfully treated, although it was rich in both gold and silver. The mine has been opened and closed a number of times. At the peak of operation from forty to sixty men worked in the mine, which had 4,000 feet of tunnels.

The Buffalo Mine, near Granite, while not a big producer, had the distinction of operating the longest period of time.

Granite is located in the northeast corner of Grant County, about fifteen miles west of Sumpter. The first man to arrive there was Harvey Robbins, on July 4, 1862, with a wagon pulled by eight head of oxen. As we travel the broad highway leading to this old mining town today, we wonder how anyone could traverse the steep canyons on foot or

Ore stacked for shipping at the California Mine near Sumpter in 1901.

Granite, Oregon, the old and the new; old Granite in the foreground.

horseback, let alone with oxen pulling a wagon. No wonder Robbins is referred to as the father of Granite!

Gold was discovered the year of Robbins' arrival. A marker is located at the foot of the hill. The town was called Independence until 1878, when an application was made for a post office. Since Oregon already had a town named Independence, it was left to the governor to select a name; his choice was Granite. The town was incorporated in 1899, with Grant Thornburg as mayor.

Granite grew like a mushroom after new mining methods and new equipment made hard-rock mining profitable. The town soon had a fine thirty-room hotel and an annex with twenty rooms, plus several smaller hotels and boardinghouses. There were also a church, a public school, a fine city water system, telephone service to the mines and to the outside world, and a covey of dance-hall girls, mining promoters, and card sharks. Four lively saloons made good business at times for the little, wooden jail. Also in sight, at the foot of the hill, was Granite's Chinatown.

There were many leading men during the boom days. Among the best known were

Express office in Granite

A McCord photograph

Old marker at foot of hill states, "Gold was discovered here July 4, 1862."

Entire families left their homes at the cry of "Gold in them thar Hills." Scene near Granite.

Courtesy Oregon Historical Society

The Black Pine placer mine was located on the north fork of the John Day River near Granite, Oregon

The Grand Hotel was built in 1900 by Grant Thornburg. It was a three-story building with 30 rooms. The hotel boasted as having an ornate bar and a fine dining room serving liquours and wines. Later Thornburg built a 20 room annex to house the crowd of incoming guests.

A McCord photograph

The Nugget Saloon and Mack & Backman's butcher shop in Granite.

A McCord photograph

The city band in Granite, Oregon in 1898. On February 27, 1900, *The Granite Gem* headlines assured the people the railroad would soon reach Granite.

Harold McCall photograph

The tiny building was Granite's first schoolhouse. The school was for a four-month period. The building also served as the Council Chambers.

Grant Thornburg, owner of the Grand Hotel, and J. N. Ditmars, a merchant succeeded by J. J. O'Dair, active for many years in the general store business.

There were exciting times. In 1900 two nuggets worth $500 and $1,800 were dug from a spring close to town. That same year Tom Eagleton was murdered by two gamblers in front of the Grand Hotel. Both gamblers shot him and both were sentenced to life.

Granite boomed for a number of years, but at last the mines began to slow down and the population drifted away. The stores,

however, continued to do a good business for a number of years — from the mines that continued to operate and from hundreds of sheep outfits summering in the area and using Granite as headquarters. For a short time gold dredges furnished a good payroll, and new equipment made it possible to recover much gold from the abandoned mine dumps. The depression years brought on a re-evaluation of gold and for a short time furnished employment for a number of men who were out of work. But the gradual slowdown caused buildings to be vacated, and Granite has now joined the ranks of full-fledged ghost towns.

Only one person has seen both the boom and the bust. This is Otis Ford, respectfully called the mayor of Granite, who has lived there all his life.

Otis has a wealth of stories. He told the writer of a miner who had reached his late eighties. The old fellow had never been sick in his life, but he was very allergic to water for bathing purposes. At last his luck ran out, and he was taken to the hospital. When he arrived, they shaved off his long, tobacco-stained beard and gave him a bath.

There was a pause as Otis sat petting his cat. Finally I asked, "What happened to him?"

Otis answered, "By God, he died. But either one was enough to kill him."

LAWTON AND ALAMO LIVED BRIEFLY

THE PRINCIPAL LODE MINES NEAR GRANITE were the Ajax, Blue Ribbon, Red Boy, Buffalo, Continental, Cougar, Independence, La Belleview, Magnolia, Monumental, and Ben Harrison.

H. E. Hendryx was editor and publisher of various newspapers in the heart of eastern Oregon's mining districts from 1897 to 1909. Later he became editor and publisher of the *Oregon Mining Review* published at Baker. Hendryx gave Oregon's Department of Geology and Mineral Industries copies of many of his newspapers. To read them is to relive Oregon's gold rush. Much of the information in this book came from their pages.

Hendryx had a lot to say about two mining towns, Lawton and Alamo, located in the Greenhorn Mountains only a short distance from Granite. Because of their short duration, they have been largely neglected in the story of Oregon's gold mining days. Their history is interesting, and without it this story wouldn't be complete.

Old Sumpter newspapers say that Lawton's site was promoted in 1900 by a Pendleton syndicate headed by James Howard. The town was three miles west of Granite at the junction of Granite and Clear Creeks in northeast Grant County and was named for Major General Henry Ware Lawton who was killed in 1899 in the Philippines.

Lots were placed on sale by the Lawton and Sumpter Real Estate and Mining Company. Two hundred people signed a peti-

tion for a post office, which opened for business in May 1900 with Frank G. Hull as postmaster.

The new town was only two miles north of the famous Red Boy Mine with its large payroll, and Lawton mushroomed. General stores and saloons were followed by other businesses. The town even had a newspaper, the *Lawton Standard,* published first in March 1900. The editor was none other than H. E. Hendryx. Wherever a new mining camp came to life, you would find Mr. Hendryx.

Daily stages connected Lawton with Baker City and waypoints. The active mines nearby were the Red Boy, Monarch, Blaine, Concord, and Congo. The town boomed for about five years, and then it was all over. The post office was discontinued in 1905.

Alamo was founded in 1899, seven miles southwest of Granite and four miles south of the Red Boy Mine.

The post office, located in the rear of Lindsay and Wade's General Store, opened in May 1900, just five days after the one in Lawton. Fred McCoy was the postmaster.

A Mr. McKee ran a thirteen-room hotel with restaurant and bar. Lloyd Judy, who now lives in Baker, tells of washing dishes and filling whiskey bottles from barrels at McKee's place when he was a boy. He later peddled milk to the miners from Thornburg's Dairy on Beaver Creek.

Alamo had three saloons, one owned by Henry Stewart who also ran the livery sta-

A McCord photograph

The Cougar and Independence Mines are located three miles north of the town of Granite and are jointly owned.

The La Belleview Mine is located in Sections 6 & T.T.8S.R.36E on Onion Creek, ten miles northeast of the town of Granite. This mine produced about $500,000 starting in 1878. There are 6,000 feet of underground works.

Dickerson placer mining camp and cook house near north fork of the John Day River, near Granite

A McCord photograph

Not even a ghost remains to tell the story of the boom days at Lawton, a mining town of short duration, located three miles west of Granite at the junction of Clear and Granite Creeks in northeast Grant County. Some 200 people, many of them families of miners working in the surrounding mines, lived here.

Old ore car with wooden wheels found in the mining area

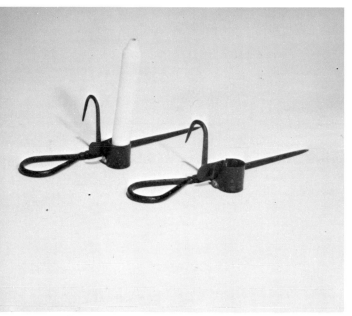

A pair of miner's candlesticks with sharp point stuck in the side of a tunnel. The candle furnished the only light for a hard-rock miner.

ble. The red-light district was not in town but over the ridge on Olive Creek. Daily stage service ran to all the towns in the mining area.

Nearby mines were the Alamo, Quebec, St. Anthony, Strausburg, Yellowstone, Van Arda, and Little Giant. Millions of dollars were invested. How much was taken out, we don't know.

As with Lawton, Alamo's life was short. The post office was discontinued in 1906. The last resident was Bill Turner, called Uncle Bill, who was both a prospector and a promoter. He continued prospecting long after there was nothing to promote.

Uncle Bill was up in years when he was found asleep in his hammock one day by a party of fishermen. Asked the name of the town, the old fellow answered indignantly, "Why, this is Alamo, and I am the mayor. You have insulted both the town and its mayor, and I have a notion to throw all of you in jail."

COPIA'S HORN OF PLENTY

THE FAMOUS CORNUCOPIA MINE GROUP — the "horn of plenty" — started operation several years after most of the big lode mines beyond the Cascade Mountains had closed down — something of a denouement to the great rushes of eastern Oregon.

The Cornucopia Mountains are located twelve miles west of Halfway in the Wallowa-Whitman National Forest. A man named Lon Simmons was among the first to discover gold in the Cornucopias in the early 1880s. Almost before he drove his last stake the mountain was crawling with men. Many prospects were made and several small producers were established, but the big mines in the area were the Union-Companion, the Last Chance, Queen of the West, and the Red Jacket.

The Last Chance was known as a pocket mine. The Union-Companion was the heavy producer reported to be on the mother lode. Because of the remoteness, poor transportation, and outdated equipment, mining was slow for a number of years. As late as the 1920s, horses were still used to haul the heavy ore wagons. Before the branch railroad came to Robinette on the Snake River, it took three days for a wagon to reach Baker.

With arrival of the railroad, electricity, and the pneumatic drill, things began to pick up. The mines were electrified in 1922 when a twenty-stamp mill was installed. It crushed sixty tons of ore a day. The stamps were like great hammers. They weighed from 1,000 to 2,000 pounds and were raised

mechanically and alternately dropped, crushing the rock so the pulverized ore could go to a chemical treatment plant where the gold was extracted.

In 1894 the Union-Companion sold for $800. In 1895 it sold again, this time for $60,000. In 1897 the mine produced $200,000, and in 1899 production reached $287,000. Later the mine sold for $700,000.[73]

The Copia mines employed 700 men during the early 1900s. The Union-Companion operated from 1884 to 1941 with a shutdown of only three years, 1927 to 1930. This group was rated among the six big mines in the United States, with thirty-six miles of tunnels. Early methods recovered only about sixty-five percent of the values. It was not until late years that fine grinding and a cyanide process saved up to ninety percent.

During the years the mines operated, the price of gold ranged from $20.67 to $35.00 a troy ounce. The total production has been reported as high as $20,000,000.

Old-timers tell of the so-called "high graders" who worked there and about the chunks of almost pure gold that found their way into boot tops and open shirts — a common practice in the early mines.

Men of many nationalities worked in the Copia mines; among them were a number of Cornishmen, known as "Cousin-Jacks." They were fine miners, having learned the trade in their home country. They were full of fun and sometimes full of beer, for they preferred it to hard liquor. When it came to

A Hazeltine photograph *Courtesy Oregon Historical Society*

The Cornucopia Mine, located ten miles northwest of Halfway in Baker County was at one time one of the six largest gold mines in the United States. It also had the longest continuous run of any mine in Oregon. There were 36 miles of tunnels and a depth of 3,000 feet. The estimated output is $20 million in combined gold, silver, copper and lead. About 300 men were employed during the heyday of operation in the late 1930s. This picture obviously was taken earlier, if mustaches and bowlers are any criterion.

Cornucopia Mine crew

A McCord photograph

In the 1920s, the Cornucopia Mines were electrified. This scene shows the miners riding to work.

Hauling boiler to the Cornucopia Mines

Union-Companion Mine of Cornucopia Mine group

Dinner time at the Union-Companion Mine of the Cornucopia group.

A McCord photograph

Five freight wagons on Main Street in Cornucopia in 1884, four years after the mines were discovered.

The dining room of the Cornucopia Mine, sometime after 1922 when the company installed its generating plant. This mine was in operation about 50 years and, before the eight-hour day went into effect, the men worked ten hours a day, seven days a week. Just think of the food that was served over these tables.

high-grading, the Cousin-Jacks were at the head of the class. They even dusted it into their hair and panned it out later. When they had made their stake it would be "So long, boys," and they were on their way back home.

Cornucopia was isolated from the outside world, due to its remoteness and the bad roads. Because of this, the miners stayed at home, creating their own fun. The Saturday night dances were always popular. Chris Schneider, who has lived in Copia for eighty years, used to play the fiddle, with his sister on piano and his nephew on drums. The Cornish miners loved to dance. They also loved fancy clothes, and their Prince Alberts and swallowtails would fly as they whirled the girls to *Sally Goodin* or *Ragtime Annie.*

As in other mining camps, Christmas and the Fourth of July were the important holidays. Labor Day was not recognized in Oregon until 1887. After that, Labor Day was *the* holiday for miners.

A shift in the early-day mines was ten hours; it was twelve hours in the mill.

Everyone worked seven days a week, so holidays were well-earned. On Labor Day, Copia was jammed with miners, ranchers, millworkers, and townspeople. By city ordinance, the saloons could serve nothing stronger than beer. That didn't bother the boys at all, for from somewhere back in the hills would come a bottled elixir of pure Pine Creek water mixed with corn squeezins, known locally as "tangle leg." A few drops would turn a pine squirrel into a screaming panther. Yet for the most part it was good clean fun, settled with bare fists and an occasional pick handle.

The Labor Day picnic lasted most of the day, followed by various contests. The tug-of-war was exciting, and much betting was carried on. There were seven men on each side, standing on two planks placed end-to-end. Cleats were spiked to the planks for good footing. At a signal from the starter the teams began to pull against each other on a rope. A red ribbon tied to the center of the rope was closely watched. Slowly it would move one way and then the other as the contestants' faces grew red and veins stood out on their necks and forearms until one team gave out. Amusements were few in those days, but one and all made the most of it.

Cornucopia was really two towns, the old and the new, the result of two different mining companies' operations. The old town was started around 1885 and had two general stores, a hotel, post office, two saloons, and a school with sixty-five pupils. The new town, about a quarter of a mile away, boasted the usual mixture of saloons, boardinghouses, and stores. School was held in an old saloon building.

Today Cornucopia would be a ghost town

Courtesy Oregon Historical Society

Entrance to the Cornucopia Mine, one of the six largest gold mines in the U.S.

were it not for a few summer homes in the area. The population in 1940, a year before the mines closed down, was 350. By 1950 only Chris Schneider and his wife remained. They are there today. Chris served several terms as mayor — a title he still holds. They are hospitable people, and they patiently answer the endless questions put to them by vacationers in the summer season.

Both the town and its fabulous gold are on the west slope of Pine Creek Canyon, north of Halfway in Baker County. From the old townsite one can see the Queen of the West and the Last Chance mines perched at an elevation of 7,000 feet on the sides of the Cornucopia Granites, where the winter snows are about seventy-five inches deep.

Dr. Waldemar Lindgren, working for the U.S. Geological Survey, stated in his report to the government in 1901:

I have never been in any mining country which I consider more promising or as having a brighter future than that of eastern Oregon. I find the mines running ten to twenty stamps which could just as well be operating fifty. They would not then be able to exhaust the ore during this or the coming generation.[73]

His report proved correct; the Cornucopia mines operated longer than any in Oregon. As late as 1938 the *Oregon Mining Journal* stated production had reached $750,000 up to November 1 of that year and from 1930 to 1938 totaled $3,000,000. Apparently there was no evidence of a slowdown, yet during World War II our government did what time, depressions, and the

elements could not do. The War Production Board's Administrative Order L-208, designed to stop the mining of noncritical metals during the war, brought a stop to all gold mining. This act caused the downfall of the Copia mines. When the war was over, deterioration within the mines, coupled with rising costs of material and higher wages, made it unprofitable to reopen.

Today, should you take the time to climb the mountain to these great mines, you can feel the silence around the darkened tunnels with their rotting timbers — the rusty ore carts standing empty on tracks that disappear into darkness. You will find yourself with strange thoughts. Before you is the evidence of over fifty years of labor — thousands of man-hours needed to build thirty-six miles of tunnels, and shafts hundreds of feet deep, dug by men into solid rock.

A short while ago the assets of the bankrupt Cornucopia Mining Company sold under the hammer for $11,100. In 1938 experts estimated that only twenty percent of the potential ore body had been extracted from the mines. A little arithmetic points to the fact that the new owner got a real bargain. If twenty percent represents $20,000,000 the remaining eighty percent represents a big profit on an $11,000 gamble. Estimates can be deceiving, but I can't think of a safer place to keep $80,000,000 — under nature's lock and key, free from taxes, deep in underground vaults. Let's call it "The Bank of Cornucopia" — the horn of plenty.

Furnace where gold sponge was formed. Each sponge is worth about $2,500 at today's prices. The sponge was heated again to form gold bricks before shipment to mint in San Francisco.

Grants Pass Art Studio photograph

Gold sponge, the last step before melting into gold bars for shipment to the mint in San Francisco. The four biscuits weigh from 250 to 300 ounces; worth about $10,000.

BOOM AND BUST

THE PERIOD BETWEEN THE LATE 1880s and 1907 could be called the boom and bust period of Oregon's lode mining. It began with the discovery of nuggets in southern Oregon in the 1850s and ten years later reached full flower in the great stampede to the land east of the Cascade Mountains. Placer or surface mining was largely hand-operated during the early years. Many of the virgin placers were very rich, and the first few years after discovery mark the high point in Oregon's gold production. Not until the easy surface pickings were gone did productive lode, or underground, mining get under way. Many rich ore veins were discovered during the early placer operations, but miners lacked the proper equipment. With poor methods of transportation, these veins were unprofitable to work.

Suddenly things changed. The stamp mill was invented, replacing the obsolete arrastra ore-crusher used since the Spanish days in Mexico. The pneumatic drill replaced the hand drill, followed by new chemical methods to extract the gold from the pulverized rock. Then came the transcontinental railroads and the Sumpter Valley Railway into the very heart of eastern Oregon's goldfields. These changes made it possible for the first time to mine with success the rich underground veins. Modern methods, coupled with Oregon's underground ore deposits, attracted wealthy investors from all over the world. They came, they saw, and they invested. Many made honest fortunes from their investments,

proving the old saying, "Prospects are found, mines are made, but it takes capital to develop a mine."

In addition to the known mines, there were many good prospects. In 1897 there were 513 known lode mines, many as yet undeveloped; by 1900 two thousand registered mines were on the books. Many of them held excellent prospects. Honest promoters and stockbrokers, as well as bankers, realized they had only scratched the surface. Experts believed the strong, well-defined veins upon which the most important mines of the region were located would continue to the greatest depths yet attained in mining. There was every reason for optimism. People from abroad were eager to buy Oregon mining stocks. Those who came to see for themselves increased their investments. Money was easy to find for a few years; the eyes of the financial world were focused on the Blue Mountain goldfields.

Trainloads of mining equipment arrived every few days at railheads near the center of the gold strike. Specially built wagons to handle the heavy boilers and other equipment were drawn by horses and mules — sometimes as many as thirty to a wagon. Mining camps were everywhere, and the mountain roads were crowded day and night. The horse-drawn stages carried people from all walks of life. The saloons and hotels were crowded with strangers looking for a bit of the action. Oregon mines were bought outright by financial giants as far

Advertisement for stock in Gold Bug Mine

away as London. Mining stocks were being sold to people rich and poor. By 1906 the entire nation was hit by a wave of speculation.

Besides the honest people selling stocks in proven Oregon mines, another group of shyster wildcat promoters sold so-called gilt-edged stocks in dry holes to millions of innocent investors. At one time the situation was so bad the governor of Pennsylvania threatened to stop the sale of Oregon mining stocks. This, in time, began to destroy the confidence of people in general. Full-page ads appeared in newspapers:

You can enter the temple of fortune by purchasing
HIAWATHA MINING STOCK
50,000 shares at 10 cents a share.

NOTE: There is no record of production and the mine is not mentioned in mining journals.

Buy STANDARD CONSOLIDATED at 12½ cents a share. Dividents are sure to follow as day succeeds night. $500,000 worth of rich ore waiting to be processed.
Company offices in Sumpter, New York, Boston, Baltimore, Philadelphia, Grand Rapids, and Dubuque.

NOTE: The records show very, very little production.

---

24 reasons why you should buy HIGHLAND mining stock at 8 cents a share.

NOTE: No record of production.

The Smuggler Gold Mining Co. in the rich Greenhorn Mountains is offering 100,000 shares at 25 cents a share.

NOTE: No record of production.

When stockholders were due at the Mountain View Mine, shotgun guards stood at the entrance to give the impression of fabulous wealth. There was *no record of production*. The little mining town of Bourne was notorious as the headquarters for schemers and wildcat operators. The most famous among them was F. Wallace

White, founder of the Sampson Company, Ltd., with offices in Bourne, New York City, and London. This company fleeced millions from people all over the world. A single printing press was hauled to Bourne by wagon. From the day it was set up, it hardly had an opportunity to cool off for six years. Two separate, distinctly different newspapers were printed on this press: One was an ordinary newspaper for local consumption; the other, with a worldwide mailing list, was sent to interested get-rich-quick suckers around the globe. A beautiful gilt-edged prospectus rolled off the press. It was perhaps Oregon's most fantastic swindle, carried on mainly through the U.S. mail. The fraudulent newspaper told of rich strikes that were never made, gold shipments that were never shipped, and ore mills that never existed.

White, through the Sampson Company, Ltd., set up a $7,000,000 corporation to buy all the big-producing mines in the Cracker Creek district and merge them under one ownership. The scheme took this form:

Capital Stock – $7,000,000.
1,400,000 shares – Par Value, $5.
Shares issued fully paid, forever nonassessable, without personal liability.
Withdrawn from public issue to pay for some of the properties and as part payment on others, under contract with owners were:
400,000 shares – $2,000,000;
Leaving in the treasury – $5,000,000.

The 1,000,000 shares were listed on the stock exchanges in London, New York, Boston, Chicago, and Salt Lake City.

How much of the $5,000,000 earmarked for the treasury went instead into Mr. White's pocket isn't known. He erected a beautiful mansion in Bourne, with lovely terraced grounds. The large living room had a massive stone fireplace and a stairway which led up six feet to a spacious dining room where exclusive full-dress dinners and fancy balls were held in all the splendor of that age.

After six years of successfully swindling

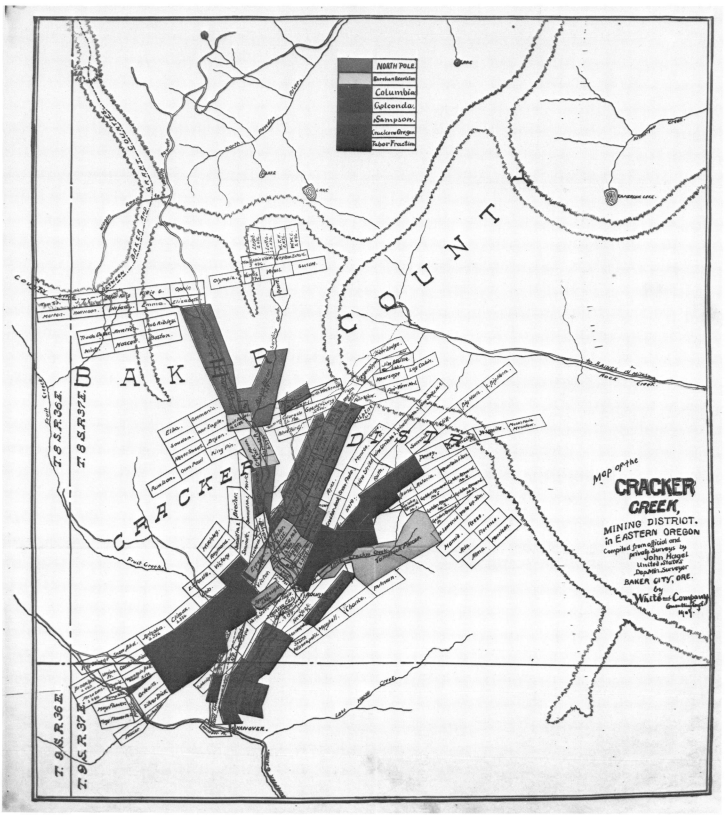

The Sampson Company, Ltd., with offices in Bourne, Oregon, in New York and London, headed by F. Wallace White, swindled the public out of $5 million in a wildcat mining stock deal. In time the government took action and Mr. White skipped out, leaving everything behind but his money. Several of Oregon's large producers are in the Cracker Creek mining district and were included in the Sampson Company scheme. Note: The mines in black on the map were included in White's stock deal.

The Risk tunnel on the Sampson mine property was 627 feet long. There is no record of production but the mine was owned by the Sampson Company, Ltd., headed by F. Wallace White, the company that swindled millions from the public. Whenever prospective mining stock buyers were to arrive at some of the mines controlled by promoters of questionable character, shotgun guards stood at the entrance to the mines to give the impression of great wealth.

Most of America's Rich Men Obtained Their Wealth from Mines—Chance for Others

How These People Made Their Money

Senator Hanna's $12,000,000 was largely derived from mines.

Senator Elkins of West Virginia is rated at $7,000,000, mostly made in the mines.

Senator Jones of Nevada is worth $10,000,000 in gold and silver mines.

McConnell from the Scranton District, worth at least $20,000,000, dug his wealth out of the mines.

Senator Clark of Montana, by all odds the richest man in Congress, worth anywhere from $100,000,000 to $500,000,000, made all his money in mines.

In 1895 Alexander Baring bought the North Pole Mine in Baker County, Oregon, from Tommy McEwen, for $10,000. Last year he dug out of it almost $1,000,000 worth of gold, and the mine to-day is said to be worth $10,000,000.

Al. Geiser of Baker City, Ore., who twelve years ago drove an express wagon, took hold of and developed a $2,000 quartz claim called the Bonanza, and six years later sold it for $500,000. Its value to-day is estimated at $3,000,000.

In October, 1898, Charles M. Reed and associates of Erie, Pa., purchased the Iron Dyke Group of Copper Claims on Snake River, Baker County, Oregon, for $50,000. In July, 1901, they were offered $2,000,000 for the property by the Mexican Trust Company.

Ten years ago Sam Ottenheimer, a merchant of Baker City, Ore., sold to Clark Tabor a half interest in the Red Boy Mine, Grant County, Oregon, for the sum of $1,000. Four years later Tabor refused $200,000 for his share of the property, and to-day it is rated at $3,000,000.

Geiser & Hendryx of Sumpter, Ore., a few weeks ago purchased a mine called the "Midway," in the Cracker Creek district, Baker County, Oregon. Since then they struck a twenty-foot ledge in the claim, averaging $38 in gold per ton. They paid $10,000 for the property, and can readily sell out for $200,000.

Old man Knapp (N. H.), up to a short time ago lived up in the mountains on Rock Creek in a tumble-down shanty on his "Highland" Group of Claims, subsisting on a little flour, and pork and beans were a luxury. Four weeks ago he sold his claim to Neil J. Sorenson & Co., of Sumpter, Ore. He now has a bank account of $45,000, and can be seen on the streets of Baker City wearing a broadcloth suit of clothes.

The Copper King Mining Claim, later rechristened as the "Spotted Horse," in the Quartzburg mining district, Grant County, Oregon, was offered eight years ago to A. W. Dunn for $500, but rejected. Since then this claim has proven to contain the only well-defined cobalt ledge in the United States, besides carrying large values in gold. For this claim and a number of surrounding ones the Clarks of Montana last year offered $500,000 but their offer was not accepted. A few weeks ago the Killen Warner Stewart Company of Sumpter, Ore., acquired control of this group under the name of the Standard Consolidated Mines Company and incorporated the same for $5,000,000.

Some two years ago G. W. Grayson, owner of the Virtue mine in Baker County, Oregon, a property that has produced several million dollars, came to the conclusion that the mine was played out and sold the plant, including a twenty-stamp mill to C. E. Gault of Montreal, Canada, for $35,000, throwing in the mine for good luck. A few weeks ago Arthur Buckbee, the manager, took out a little batch of ore that contained $40,000 worth of gold; one chunk weighing ninety pounds gave mint returns of $14,000.

12

Excerpts from beautiful pamphlets produced by promoters of mining stock such as this were mailed everywhere. They were even given to passengers on west bound trains.

the public, White began to show signs of uneasiness, and for good reason — by that time, Uncle Sam was breathing down his neck. One night he disappeared, never to return, leaving everything but his money. His departure was well-timed; the sheriff was only one step behind him. Bourne never recovered. As for White, he continued to operate various swindles until he was finally convicted of mail fraud, a charge he had avoided for so long.

White was only one of many swindlers who helped tarnish the gilt on Oregon mining stocks. It was unfortunate that this came at a time of over-speculation all across the nation, ending in the Panic of 1907. On October 22, the Knickerbocker Trust Company in New York, with deposits of $48,000,000 closed its doors. This caused runs on other companies. Investigation disclosed a deficit of required reserves in New York banks alone totaling $38,838,825. The stock market scare panicked bankers everywhere, so that no money could be borrowed by speculators or legitimate mine operators. When the source of money dried up, the mines, both good and bad, were forced to slow down. In most cases they closed . In the end it was the fast-buck boys who killed the goose that was laying the golden eggs.

This was the end of the boom days, but it was by no means the end of gold mining in Oregon. It did, however, produce a costly slowdown in lode or underground mining from which the prospector and small operators never recovered. Many of Oregon's larger mines closed, later to be faced with the high cost of reopening. Rotted timbers had to be replaced and cave-ins cleared from the tunnels. In most cases expensive pumping operations were necessary to clear the bores of accumulated water. Mining experts say it costs more to open a closed mine than to build a new one.

Pictures showing early-day gold mining stocks as they were presented to the public. Some were legitimate, others were not worth the paper they were written on, and it was the promoters and shysters that killed the goose that laid the golden egg.

From the Numismatist.   From the coin catalog.

When the mines closed down in 1907 due to over speculation, money was so scarce that the citizens of Baker, Oregon issued gold slugs of native gold. Each was worth $40. On one side of the coin it read, "Baker City 2 ounces." On the other side, "In Gold We Trust." The government soon put a stop to it. At first a few sold for $900 at auction, but coin dealers valued them as high as $3,000 each.

Full page ads such as these appeared in newspapers. There is no record of production from any of these

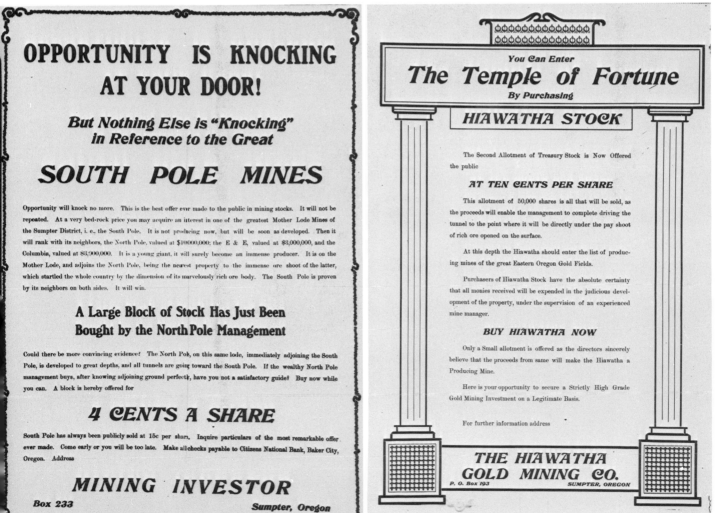

OPPORTUNITY IS KNOCKING AT YOUR DOOR!

But Nothing Else is "Knocking" in Reference to the Great

SOUTH POLE MINES

Opportunity will knock no more. This is the best offer ever made to the public in mining stocks. It will not be repeated. At a very bed-rock price you may acquire an interest in one of the greatest Mother Lode Mines of the Sumpter District, i. e., the South Pole. It is not producing now, but will be soon as developed. Then it will rank with its neighbors, the North Pole, valued at $10000,000; the E & E, valued at $3,000,000, and the Columbia, valued at $3,900,000. It is a young giant, it will surely become an immense producer. It is on the Mother Lode, and adjoins the North Pole, being the nearest property to the immense ore shoot of the latter, which startled the whole country by the dimension of its marvelously rich ore body. The South Pole is proven by its neighbors on both sides. It will win.

A Large Block of Stock Has Just Been Bought by the North Pole Management

Could there be more convincing evidence? The North Pole, on this same lode, immediately adjoining the South Pole, is developed to great depths, and all tunnels are going toward the South Pole. If the wealthy North Pole management buys, after knowing adjoining ground perfectly, have you not a satisfactory guide? Buy now while you can. A block is hereby offered for

4 CENTS A SHARE

South Pole has always been publicly sold at 15c per share. Inquire particulars of the most remarkable offer ever made. Come early or you will be too late. Make all checks payable to Citizens National Bank, Baker City, Oregon. Address

MINING INVESTOR

Box 233   Sumpter, Oregon

You Can Enter
The Temple of Fortune
By Purchasing

HIAWATHA STOCK

The Second Allotment of Treasury Stock is Now Offered the public

AT TEN CENTS PER SHARE

This allotment of 50,000 shares is all that will be sold, as the proceeds will enable the management to complete driving the tunnel to the point where it will be directly under the pay shoot of rich ore opened on the surface.

At this depth the Hiawatha should enter the list of producing mines of the great Eastern Oregon Gold Fields.

Purchasers of Hiawatha Stock have the absolute certainty that all monies received will be expended in the judicious development of the property, under the supervision of an experienced mine manager.

BUY HIAWATHA NOW

Only a Small allotment is offered as the directors sincerely believe that the proceeds from same will make the Hiawatha a Producing Mine.

Here is your opportunity to secure a Strictly High Grade Gold Mining Investment on a Legitimate Basis.

For further information address

THE HIAWATHA GOLD MINING CO.
P. O. Box 193   SUMPTER, OREGON

It was unfortunate that this happened just when the lode mines' future looked so bright. With the rising cost of labor and material, and with a continued shortage of capital, Oregon's underground mines simply had to wait for more favorable conditions, for it is true that "where there is gold, men will find a way."

Money was so short that local citizens and bankers banded together and issued slugs of native gold. These did not bear the government stamp but were worth their weight in gold. On one side of the coin it read *"Baker City 2 ounces"* and on the other *"In Gold We Trust."* It wasn't long before the federal government got wind of this money-making scheme and ordered the guilty parties to cease and desist, but the slugs climbed in value as collectors' items. Originally sold at auctions for about $900, coin dealers later valued them at $3,000.

From 1908 through 1912 gold production was cut fifty percent. A large share of the ore that was produced came from placer mines, which a poor man could work without expensive equipment. To make a living, many hard-rock miners out of a job turned to placer diggings.

A new, largely experimental type of mining had started in Oregon as early as 1900 — the floating bucket-line dredge. The dredge is installed in stream beds, scooping up quantities of gold-bearing material which is processed onboard. The gold is extracted, and the waste (called tailings) is left along the streams in the form of huge piles of gravel.

In 1903 a steam-powered dredge began operation on Foot's Creek in southwestern Oregon.[75] It was not until 1913, however, that the first of several large dredges began working in Sumpter Valley. This became the largest dredge field in the state, so successful that by the end of the year Oregon's placer gold production more than doubled. In 1916 it nearly doubled again when dredging began along the John Day River.

Mechanical dredging equipment continued to be successful, to the extent that placer mining by 1921 exceeded lode mining and continued to do so until 1954.[75]

In the Great Depression of 1929, when many men were out of work, materials and labor costs dropped back into line with gold prices, causing an upsurge in all types of gold mining. Then in 1934 the price of gold was revalued at $35.00 an ounce, bringing on a mild boom in the industry. The output for the seven years 1935 to 1941 averaged $3,000,000 per year. In 1940 gold and silver production reached $4,124,883, the highest since the early placer days of the 1860s. The 1940 output came from 112 lode mines and 192 placer mines. Actually, sixty-two percent of the gold output in Oregon that year was produced by eight properties — the Cornucopia Gold Mines, Inc. (lode), Sumpter Valley Dredging Company (bucket dredge), North-West Development Company (dredge), Porter and Company (dredge), Ferris Mining Company (dredge), Lewis Investment Company (lode), Timms Gold Dredging Company (dredge), and B & H Company (dredge).[75]

Oregon's gold mining virtually ceased when war Production Board Order L-208 was put into effect in 1942. This curtailed the average yearly production from $3,000,000 to $55,400.[75] Placer mining may never recover, since much of the best placer ground has been exhausted. The shortage of available water is another problem. New laws concerned with the environment must now also be considered. But little doubt exists among mining men that the great bulk of Oregon's underground gold is still there, locked deep in the earth.

It would take millions to develop a lode mine today, so don't expect a modern-day gold rush, with men digging along the creeks and streams with pick and shovel. However, the rapid upsurge in the international price of gold, coupled with inflation, has brought renewed interest among both amateurs and professionals in searching for gold in the Oregon fields and in California's mother lode. Occasionally there are rich finds — a pair of modern-day prospectors discovered a nugget worth an estimated $50,000 in the Yuba River country in California. But most of the well-defined veins are already known. It will take new scientific methods to reduce the costs enough to realize a profit.

It has been said many times that there are more treasures in the mountains than were ever taken out. And, as we all know, history has a way of repeating itself. Adlai Stevenson once remarked, "We can't just look back to great yesterdays, we must look forward to greater tomorrows."

Oregon State Highway photograph

Courtesy Oregon Historical Society

Old-timer showing tenderfoot would-be miners how to use a goldpan

GOLD BLAZED THE WAY

HOW MUCH GOLD WAS REALLY PRODUCED IN OREGON? The U.S. Bureau of Mines Yearbook reports that Oregon's total production from 1852 to 1965 was $130,822,000. The heaviest production years on the Pacific Coast date from 1849, with the discovery of gold in California, to about 1880. These were the years when the virgin treasure was found close to the surface. It called for placer mining, which required less capital. Lode or underground mining came later, at a time when the surface gold was nearly gone. However, during the years of heavy production the government kept no accounting. Record-keeping was not started until 1880* Therefore, early-day statistics of gold production were meager and for the most part were based on records of Wells Fargo, banks, post offices, and steamer shipments to the U.S. Mint.

It is interesting to note that the Director of the Mint credits Oregon with only $16,816,275 in gold from 1852 to June 30, 1882, a period of thirty years. A June 1963 article written by F. W. Libbey in *The Ore-Bin*, published by the Oregon State Department of Geology and Mineral Industries, estimated that from 1852 to 1862 (a period of only ten years) southern Oregon produced $31,200,000 — double the amount the Director of the Mint credited to all of Oregon for a period of thirty years.

Gold was discovered in southern Oregon in 1850 and 1851. Report No. 58 of the *California State Geologist* showed that California produced $41,273,106 in gold in 1850, $75,938,232 in 1851, and $81,294,700 in 1852. *The very year gold was discovered in Oregon, California's production almost doubled, by their own figures.*

No established boundary line existed between the two states. It was a case of "So what? It's all gold, and who cares where it came from?" At least half of the Oregon miners were from California and no doubt carried their gold back home with them, as they did ten years later during the gold rush to the Pacific Northwest. F. W. Libbey estimates the total production from southern Oregon to 1961 as $69,544,000 — quite a substantial total compared to figures of the U.S. Mint.

Gold discovered in eastern Oregon and the Pacific Northwest in 1861 and 1862 caused Philip H. Parrish in his *Historic Oregon* to write: "Out of the Pacific mines came gold to pay for the Civil War." From 1861 to 1867 the Pacific Northwest produced $140,000,000 while California was producing $210,000,000, according to "Pioneer Stimulus of Gold" by Leslie M. Scott and W. J. Trimble in *Mining Advance*, published by the University of Wisconsin.*

It is unfortunate that many historians and writers in general have never given Oregon credit for the actual amount of gold pro-

---

*Government figures since then are considered to be accurate.

*Bulletin 3, No. 2, p. 73

duced in the state. Trimble observed, "Eastern Oregon mines seem scarcely to have received the attention that their importance in building up that part of the state warrants." *The Ore-Bin* in May 1939 said, "Oregon does not have the reputation of a mining state among those who are not well informed on the subject."

Unfortunately for southern Oregon, no government geologists covered those early mining days. However, when gold was discovered in eastern Oregon in 1861-1862 it was not long until two mining experts were on the job: R. W. Raymond, U.S. Commissioner of Mining, and Dr. Waldemar Lindgren of the U.S. Geological Survey.

Oregon has been credited with producing $20,000,000 in gold from 1861 to 1867, yet Lindgren estimated that the production for only four of those six years was close to $50,000,000.[76] All figures show that early-day placers were very rich and that the first few years after discovery marked the high point in gold production. Report 58 of the *California State Geologist* from 1848 to 1963 distinctly shows this; accordingly, it is reasonable to think that Oregon's production from 1861 to 1867 should have been nearer $75,000,000 than the $20,000,000 with which the state is credited.

The *Oregon Mining Review* in July 1939 stated that from 1861 to 1900 eastern Oregon produced $100,000,000 in gold. *Lest We Forget* by Libby credits southern Oregon with $50,000,000 from 1852 to 1901. The new book *Gold and Silver in Oregon* by the Oregon State Department of Geology and Mineral Industries places Oregon's production at $66,382,147 from 1900 to 1965. This would give Oregon a grand total of $216,382,147 — a much more reasonable figure than the 130,822,000 credited by the Bureau of Mines.

I have examined every available record over a period of four years, taking into consideration the estimates and opinions of experts such as Raymond, Lindgren, and many others, rather than drawing conclusions from articles produced by so-called historians. Dr. Lindgren is held in high esteem as a geologist, and his findings would appear quite conclusive. Therefore, from my extensive study it is my opinion that *Oregon's total gold production should be even higher than that recorded by either the Bureau of Mines or the State of Oregon.* It raises the point: Had the U.S. Mint been located in the Pacific Northwest rather than in San Francisco, would the production records have been different?

When all is said and done, it's not the amount of gold that came from an area that's really important. What is important is that the gold miner opened the gates to the wilderness and, in doing so, helped to settle most of the land west of the Rocky Mountains.

The prospector built his lonely cabin on the mountain among the pines. Lulled to sleep at night by the music of the brook, he dreamed he had struck it rich. He cried out in his sleep, "I've struck it, I've struck it," and the bullfrog in the meadow echoed back, "Struck it, struck it."

People coming to this lovely land today might well cry out, "I've struck it, I've struck it."

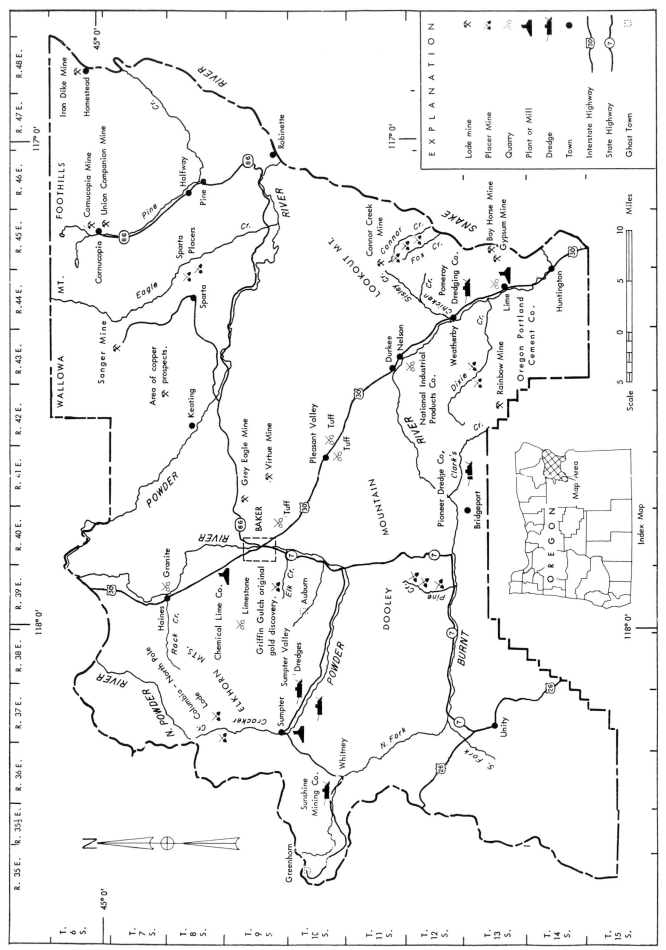

Baker County showing location of principal mines 1861-1959

EXPLANATION

Lode mine
Placer Mine
Quarry
Plant or Mill
Dredge
Town
Interstate Highway
State Highway
Ghost Town

Index Map

Map Area

OREGON

Scale

Miles

Iron Dike Mine
Homestead
Cornucopia Mine
Union Companion Mine
FOOTHILLS
Cornucopia
Halfway
Pine
WALLOWA MT.
Sanger Mine
Sparta Placers
Sparta
Area of copper prospects.
Keating
Robinette
POWDER RIVER
Grey Eagle Mine
Virtue Mine
Tuff
BAKER
Tuff
Pleasant Valley
Tuff
Tuff
Connor Creek Mine
Bay Horse Mine
Gypsum Mine
Pomeroy Dredging Co.
Durkee
Nelson
Weatherby
National Industrial Products Co.
Lime
Oregon Portland Cement Co.
Huntington
Rainbow Mine
LOOKOUT MT.
SNAKE RIVER
BURNT RIVER
Granite
Haines
Columbia - North pole Lode
Chemical Lime Co.
Limestone
Griffin Gulch original gold discovery.
Auburn
Sumpter Valley
Dredges
ELKHORN MTS.
N. POWDER RIVER
Cracker Cr.
Whitney
Sunshine Mining Co.
Greenhorn
DOOLEY MOUNTAIN
POWDER
N. Fork
Pioneer Dredge Co., Clark's Cr.
Bridgeport
Unity
N

R. 35 E. | R. 35½ E. | R. 36 E. | R. 37 E. | R. 38 E. | R. 39 E. | R. 40 E. | R. 41 E. | R. 42 E. | R. 43 E. | R. 44 E. | R. 45 E. | R. 46 E. | R. 47 E. | R. 48 E.

118° 0'
117° 0'
45° 0'

T. 6 S. | T. 7 S. | T. 8 S. | T. 9 S. | T. 10 S. | T. 11 S. | T. 12 S. | T. 13 S. | T. 14 S. | T. 15 S.

NOTES AND BIBLIOGRAPHY

THE MAIN OBJECT in preparing this book has been to record the history of gold mining in Oregon and to emphasize the effects of mining and miners upon the growth and economy of the state.

To accomplish this, I have relied heavily upon state and local publications such as the *Oregon Historical Quarterly* published by the Oregon Historical Society (which for identification will abbreviated O.H.Q.) and books dealing with Oregon's history from pioneer days such as *The History of the Oregon Country* by Leslie Scott; pioneer diaries and reminiscences; microfilm at the Multnomah County Library and the Oregon State archives, Salem; Professor Waldemar Lindgren's *Gold Fields of Eastern Oregon* in U.S. Department of the Interior 22nd Annual Report to Congress, June 30, 1901; R. W. Raymond 1870-77, *Statistics of Mines and Mining West of the Rocky Mountains*, U.S. Treasury Department Annual Reports;

J. R. Browne 1867-69, *Reports on Mineral Resources of the U.S. West of Rocky Mountains*, U.S. Treasury Department; *The Ore-Bin*, published by the Oregon State Department of Geology and Mineral Industries; *Gold and Silver in Oregon*, published by the Oregon State Department of Geology and Mineral Industries.

Because of considerable overlapping of history covering Oregon, the Pacific Northwest, and the entire Pacific Coast, and in order to bring some coherence, I have relied upon regional history as well.

A numbering system has been used throughout the book. A corresponding number covering the source of the material is located here in the bibliography. Other source material is also located here but is not numbered. The two groups, numbered and unnumbered, cover the complete historical documents from which the story *Oregon's Golden Years* was compiled.

NUMBERED BIBLIOGRAPHY

1. *Opening Highway to the Pacific*, O.H.Q., by James Christy Bell, Jr.
2. *Stephen Hall Meek: Autobiography of a Mountain Man 1805 to 1889* by Glenn Dawson.
3. *Terrible Trail: The Meek Cut Off* by Keith Clark and Lowell Tiller, Caxton Printers, Caldwell, Idaho, 1966; *Fort Boise Story: Oregon Trail* by F. G. Young, O.H.Q., Vol. 1, December 1900.
4. O.H.Q., Vol. XLI:I, story by George Himes, Sept. 3; *Field Diary*, O.H.Q.
5. *Route of Meek's Cut Off* by Lawrence A. McNary, O.H.Q., Vol. 35.
6. *History of Oregon* by Bancroft, Vol. 2, pp. 194-204; *History of Oregon Country* by Leslie Scott, Vol. II.
7. *History of Oregon Country* by Leslie Scott, Vol. III, "Where Is the Blue Bucket Mine?" taken from the Helm diary, Appendix pp. 336-338.
8. *History of Oregon* by Bancroft, Vol. 1, p. 512.
9. *U.S. Dept. of the Interior, 22nd Annual Report to Congress*, June 30, 1901, U.S. Geological Survey, "Gold Fields of Eastern Oregon" by Prof. Waldemar Lindgren; *Gold Fields of Eastern Oregon* by P. Donan, O. R. & N. Co., Portland, 1900.
10. *The Early Indian Wars of the West* by Francis Victor, Salem, 1894; *Land of the Giants* by David Lavender.
11. *Records of the 34th Congress*, 3rd Session, Vol. 1, part 2, p. 169.
12. O.H.Q., Vol. 4, by Henry E. Reed (45 soldiers at The Dalles, 1861; 127 at Fort Walla Walla).
13. *History of Oregon Country* by Leslie Scott.
14. O.H.Q., Vol. LX, No. 4, by Edward R. Payne, post office information "Wascopum."
15. *History of Oregon Country* by Leslie Scott; *Roads and Transportation of Territorial Oregon*, O.H.Q., Vol. XLI, 1940, pp. 40-52; *Glimpses of Early Days in Oregon* by C. M. Cartwright, O.H.Q., Vol. IV, Mar. 1903; *History of Willamette Valley*, O.H.Q., 1927, by Robert C. Clark.
16. *Reminiscences of Seventy Years*, O.H.Q., Vol. XIII, Sept. 1912, by John K. Barlow.
17. *Pictorial History of Southern Oregon and Northern California* by Jack Sutton.
18. *History of Oregon Country* by Leslie Scott; *Land of the Giants* by David Lavender.
19. *Opening Highway to the Pacific*, O.H.Q., by James Christy Bell.
20. *History of Oregon Country* by Leslie Scott; *Land of the Giants* by David Lavender.
21. *Oregon Oddities No. 5*, Farm Life, p. 4.
22. *Columbia River Men in California, 1848-49*, O.H.Q., by Wm. M. Case, Vol. 2, p. 169.
23. *Early Southern Oregon*, O.H.Q., Vol. 19, by Binger Herman; *History Placer Mining in Oregon*, 1939, by August Spreen (Note: Copy in office, Oregon State Geological Office, Portland); *Gold and Silver in Oregon* by State of Oregon Dept. of Geology and Mineral Industries; *The Golden Frontier* by Reinhard (Texas); *Lest We Forget* by F. W. Libbey, Oregon Dept. Geology, Vol. 25, No. 6.
24. *Early Southern Oregon* by Binger Herman; *Pictorial History of Southern Oregon and Northern California* by Jack Sutton.
25. *History Placer Mining in Oregon* by August Spreen, 1939.
26. *Lest We Forget* by F. W. Libbey.
27. *First Stage Line from Portland to Sacramento* (Pictorial History) by Jack Sutton; *Stage Line Portland to Sacramento*, O.H.Q., Vol. 35, pp. 131-138, by Osborn Winther.
28. *Ancient River Beds*, Oregon Papers, Vol. XI and XII by D. H. Stearns.
29. *Gold on Sterling Creek* by Francis D. Hains and Vern S. Smith; *Lest We Forget* by F. W. Libbey, Oregon Dept. Geology.
30. *Dodges History*.
31. *Handbook of the Mining Industry of Oregon* by Parks and Swartler, Oregon Bureau Mines and Geology, mineral resources of Oregon, Vol. 2, No. 4, p. 306.
32. *Mineral Resources of Southwest Oregon* (Diller), U.S. Geological Survey, Bull. 546, p. 147.
33. Briggs Pocket mentioned in *Gold and Silver in Oregon*.
34. *Mineral Resources of Southwest Oregon* (Diller), U.S. Geological Survey, Bull. 546, p. 147.
35. *Handbook of the Mining Industry of Oregon* by Parks and Swartler, Oregon Bureau Mines and Geology, 1916.
36. *The Greenback Mine Southern Oregon* by Parks and Swartler; *The Ashland Mine*, Burch, 1942, pp. 105-128, O.H.Q., Vol. 43, No. 2.
37. *Lest We Forget*, F. W. Libbey; *Ore-Bin*, Vol. 25, June 1963, pp. 93-109.
38. *California Report No. 58, California Division of Mines*, Ferry Bldg., San Francisco.
39. *Oregon Oddities No. 5*, Farm Life, p. 4.
40. *When Oregon Became a State*, O.H.Q., Vol. LX, No. 4, by Edward R. Payne.
41. *Currency Question in Oregon During Civil War*, O.H.Q., Vol. 28, 1927, by Joseph Ellison.

42. "The Story of Portland" in *History of Oregon Country* by Leslie Scott, Vol. III; "The Story of Portland" in *History Columbia River Valley: The Dalles to the Sea* by Fred Lockley; "The Story of Portland" in *History of Oregon and Pacific Northwest* by Parrish; "The Story of Portland" in *Oregon End of the Trail*, Federal Writers Project; *Stage Line Portland to Sacramento*, O.H.Q., Vol. 35, pp. 131-138, by Osborn Winther; *Land of the Giants* by David Lavender; O.H.Q., Vol. LX, No. 4, by Edward Payne about post office, etc.; *Works of Stewart Holbrook*; *Oregon in the Making* by Barzee; *The Portland Story*, O.H.Q., Vol. 14, 1913, by Thomas Prosch; *History of Oregon* by Bancroft, Vol. 2, 1880 (141 seagoing ships in Portland and Astoria Harbor); *Oregon Geographic Names* by McArthur; *Centennial History of Oregon 1811-1911* by Joseph Gaston.

43. *History of Oregon Country* by Leslie Scott; *History of Oregon*, O.H.Q., by Robert Platt; *31 Years in Baker County* by Isaac Hiatt; *Illustrated History Baker, Grant, Malheur and Harney Counties* by Western Historical Publishing Company, 1902 (also see page 786; also Chapter VII); *History of Oregon* by Bancroft, Vols. 1 and 2; *Oregon End of the Trail*, Federal Writers Project.

44. *History of Oregon County* by Leslie Scott, Appendix pp. 330-348.

45. Story about Auburn in *31 Years in Baker County* by Isaac Hiatt, 1861-1893; *History of Oregon* by Bancroft, Vol. 2, p. 479; *Washington Statesman*, newspaper, Walla Walla, July 20, 1862; *Bedrock Democrat*, early-day Baker newspaper; *The Oregonian*, April 29, 1864, June 8, 1863, October 7, 1863; *Illustrated History Baker, Grant, Malheur and Harney Counties* by Western Historical Publishing Company, 1902.

46. *History of The Dalles*, O.H.Q., Vol. LX, No. 4, by Edward R. Payne; *Empire of the Columbia* by Johansen; *History Columbia River Valley: The Dalles to the Sea* by Fred Lockley; *Opening Highway to the Pacific 1838-1846*, O.H.Q., by James Christy Bell; *Oregon End of the Trail*, Federal Writers Project; *History of The Dalles 1870*, Oregon folks, pp. 159-160, in the newspaper "Washington Statesman," Walla Walla, Aug. 18, 1872; *Reminiscences of Eastern Oregon* by Mrs. Elizabeth Lord; *History Wasco County* by Wm. H. McNeal, The Dalles; O.H.Q., Vol. 5, 1904, by P. W. Gillette (number settlers living beyond the Deschutes River); O.H.Q., Vol. 16, 1915, by T. C. Elliott; *The Dalles Mountaineer*, early-day newspaper.

47. *Oregon First Monopoly, The O.S.N. Co.*, O.H.Q., Vol. 9, by Irene L. Poppleton; *Lure of the River*, O.H.Q., Vol. XXX, March 1933, by Fred Wilson; *Transporting Livestock Up River by Boat*, O.H.Q., Vol. 50, 1949, by Earl Stewart, O.H.Q., Vol. XLI, 1940, pp. 40-52; *Inland Empire of Pacific Northwest* by Fuller, Vol. III, 1928; *Historic Oregon* by Parrish (82,000 people up river by boat in three years, miners and homesteaders; 30,000 engaged in mining, 1862); *History of Oregon Country* by Leslie Scott, pp. 330-348; *A Brief History of Oregon Steam & Navigation Company*, O.H.Q., 1904, by P. W. Gillette, The Dalles wharf; *The Roads and Transportation of Territorial Oregon*, O.H.Q., Vol. XL, 1940, pp. 40-52; *The Portland Story* by Stewart Holbrook; *River Boats* by Stewart Holbrook; *The Oregonian*: Gold rush days up river, Sept. 23, 1861, March 18, 1862, June 27, 1862, Aug. 7, Sept. 8,
Nov. 16, Feb. 11 and Feb. 14, 1865; *Oregon and Pacific Northwest* by Lancaster Pollard; *Oregon Folks* in the newspaper "Washington Statesman," Walla Walla, Aug. 18, 1862, pp. 49-61 (story about trail Canyon City to The Dalles).

48. *Illustrated History Baker, Grant, Malheur and Harney Counties* by Western Historical Publishing Company, 1902,; *History of the Express Company* by A. L. Stimson; O.H.Q., Vol. 4, by Henry E. Reed (about soldiers in the area); "Gold Fields of Canyon City," diary of Ralph Fisk in *Oregon End of the Trail*, Federal Writers Project; *Gold Fields of Eastern Oregon* by Dr. Waldemar Lindgren; *History Placer Mining in Oregon* by August Spreen, 1939; *The Blue Mountain Eagle*, early-day John Day newspaper; *Gold and Silver in Oregon* by Oregon State Dept. of Geology and Mineral Industries.

49. *Gold by Mail* in The Oregonian, Sept. 14, Sept. 16, Oct. 30, 1865.

50. *History of Oregon Country* by Leslie Scott.

51. *U.S. Dept. of the Interior, 22nd Annual Report to Congress*, June 30, 1901, U.S. Geological Survey, Prof. Waldemar Lindgren, pp. 636-717.

52. *Statistics of Mining West of Rocky Mountains*, Doc. No. 10, Serial Congressional Report No. 1811, p. 181; also Doc. No. 207, Serial No. 1424, p. 224, by R. W. Raymond.

53. *Blue Mountain Eagle*, Centennial Edition, John Day.

54. *Chinamen Laws in Oregon*, O.H.Q., Vol. 8, 1907, F. G. Young; *Chinese Laws*, Oregon State Constitution, Article XV, Sec. 8, Sept. 18, 1857, also Oregon Laws 1845 to 1864, p. 815, and Oregon Laws 1869, pp. 49-50; "Chinese Tax" in *History of Oregon* by Bancroft, Vol. 2, p. 741.

55. *Gold Fields of Eastern Oregon* by P. Donan.

56. "Gold Fields of Canyon City," diary of Ralph Fisk in *Oregon End of the Trail*, Federal Writers Project.

57. *Gold Fields of Eastern Oregon* by P. Donan.

58. *Bedrock Democrat*, early-day Baker newspaper; *Blue Mountain American*, early-day Sumpter paper.

59. *31 Years in Baker County* by Isaac Hiatt.

60. *The Great Northwest*, O.H.Q., Vol. 35, pp. 131-138, by Osborn Winther (says Baker City grew up around a quartz mill).

61. *Early Southern Oregon*, O.H.Q., Vol. 19, by Binger Herman; *History Placer Mining in Oregon*, 1939, by August Spreen; *Gold and Silver in Oregon* by State of Oregon Dept. of Geology and Mineral Industries; *The Golden Frontier* by Reinhard (Texas); *Lest We Forget* by F. W. Libbey, Oregon Dept. of Geology, Vol. 25, No. 6.

62. *Goldfields of Eastern Oregon* by P. Donan, 1900, O. R. & N. Co., Portland.

63. *31 Years in Baker County* by Isaac Hiatt.

64. *31 Years in Baker County* by Isaac Hiatt, 1861-1893; *History of Oregon* by Bancroft, Vol. 2, p. 479; *Washington Statesman*, newspaper, Walla Walla; *Bedrock Democrat*, early-day Baker newspaper; *The Oregonian*; *Illustrated History Baker, Grant, Malheur and Harney Counties* by Western Historical Publishing Company, 1902.

65. *Baker County Sketch Book* by Gordon and Patricia Stewart.

66. *Illustrated History Baker, Grant, Malheur and Harney Counties* by Western Historical Publishing Company, 1902; *History of the Express Company* by A. L.

Stimson; O.H.Q., Vol. 4, by Henry E. Reed; *Oregon End of the Trail*, Federal Writers Project; *Gold Fields of Eastern Oregon* by Dr. Waldemar Lindgren; *History Placer Mining in Oregon* by August Spreen, 1939; *Gold and Silver in Oregon* by Oregon State Dept. of Geology and Mineral Industries.

67. *Oregon Papers*, Vol. XI and XII, by D. H. Stearns (tells about ancient riverbeds).

68. *U.S. Dept of the Interior, 22nd Annual Report to Congress*, June 30, 1901, U.S. Geological Survey, Prof. Waldemar Lindgren.

69. *31 Years in Baker County* by Isaac Hiatt; *History of Oregon* by Bancroft; *Illustrated History Baker, Grant, Malheur and Harney Counties* by Western Historical Publishing Company, 1902.

70. *Illustrated History Baker, Grant, Malheur and Harney Counties* by Western Historical Publishing Company, 1902; *History of the Express Company* by A. L. Stimson; O.H.Q., Vol. 4, by Henry E. Reed; *Oregon End of the Trail*, Federal Writers Project; *Gold Fields of Eastern Oregon* by Dr. Waldemar Lindgren; *History Placer Mining in Oregon* by August Spreen, 1939;

Gold and Silver in Oregon by Oregon State Dept. of Geology and Mineral Industries.

71. *Pardee and Hewett*, p. 10.

72. *Goldfields of Eastern Oregon* by P. Donan, O. R. & N. Co., Portland, 1900.

73. *U.S. Dept of the Interior, 22nd Annual Report to Congress*, June 30, 1901, U.S. Geological Survey by Prof. Waldemar Lindgren.

74. *Numismatist:* Magazine on coins; *Ore-Bin*, April 1953.

75. *Early Southern Oregon*, O.H.Q., Vol. 19, by Binger Herman; *History Placer Mining in Oregon*, 1939, by August Spreen; *Gold and Silver in Oregon* by State of Oregon Dept. of Geology and Mineral Industries; *The Golden Frontier* by Reinhard (Texas); *Lest We Forget* by F. W. Libbey, Oregon Dept. Geology, Vol. 25, No. 6.

76. *U.S. Dept. of the Interior, 22nd Annual Report to Congress*, June 30, 1901, U.S. Geological Survey, "Gold Fields of Eastern Oregon" by Prof. Waldemar Lindgren.

UNNUMBERED BIBLIOGRAPHY

The History of the Oregon Country by Leslie Scott, states there were 30,000 men mining in the Pacific Northwest by the end of 1862; Appendix pp. 330-348.

Fuller's Inland Empire of the Pacific Northwest, Vol. III, 1928, story regarding the upper portage on Columbia River.

Corning's Dictionary of Oregon History, Portage information says 1,500 to 2,000 lbs. gold came down Columbia River each week by steamer.

Field's Diary, September 3rd, states Stephen Meek told the members of wagon train at Fort Boise that he would follow up the Malheur River and down the John Day River to the Columbia River.

History of Oregon by Bancroft, Vol. 2, p. 758, Oregon wool crop in 1887 was 12,534,485 lbs. and most came from Eastern Oregon; p. 741 Chinese Tax.

Parrish Historic Oregon, 82,000 people went up the Columbia River by steamer in 3 yrs.; 24,500 in 1862, 22,000 in 1863, and 36,000 in 1864.

Empire of the Columbia by Johnson, 900-foot wharf at The Dalles.

Early Days in Oregon by Judson.

History Columbia River Valley: The Dalles to the Sea by Fred Lockley. Story regarding the Crosby house in Portland, Vol. I, P. 410.

History of Oregon Country by Scott, Vol. III, about last horse stage Portland to Sacramento 1887. Scott states between 1861-1867 Pacific Northwest produced $140,000,000 gold and California $210,000,000.

History of Oregon Country by Scott, Vol. III, pp. 61-67 says it was 1865 before Portland population reached 6,000.

Lost Mines and Treasures of Pacific Northwest by Ruby Hult.

Oregon State Archives, Salem, Oregon, microfilm and files on the Blue Bucket Mine.

O.H.Q., Vol. 13-1912, by Clarence Bagley, Steamer *Columbia* first mail steamer 1850, once monthly to six weeks; telephone line to Portland 1864.

O.H.Q., Vol. 16-1915, by Eliott, tells about old Fort Walla Walla at mouth of Walla Walla River erected by Hudson's Bay Company 1818; Fort moved to new site of Walla Walla; old site name changed to Wallula in 1858.

History of Oregon by Bancroft, Vol. 2,-1880, tells of 141 seagoing vessels in Portland and Astoria harbors.

Livestock transported by boat, O.H.Q., by Earl K. Stewart.

Armstrong Nugget, story of finding, in Sumpter Newspaper *Blue Mountain American*, June 26, 1913;

found by George Armstrong and D. I. Stewart on Buck Creek near Susanville.

Oregon Mining Journal 1940, says $50,000 from one small pocket on Carpenter claim on Olive Creek, 1860s and 1870s.

The Oregonian, November 1, 1903, Blue Bucket mine description identical with Canyon City.

Old Timers Talk by Ted Raynor.

Oregon Eldorado by Norberg, Oregon's forgotten gold.

Oregon Geographic Names by McArthur.

National Archives, Washington, D.C., post office information.

O.H.Q., Vol. 5-1904, by P. W. Gillette, says no settlers living beyond Deschutes River 1855.

O.H.Q., Vol. 16-1915, p. 133, by T. C. Elliott, Letters cost 40 cents; steamers averaged 200 passengers trip; $50,000 in tickets sold on up-river boats in March, April, May; steamer *Tenino* took in $18,000 one trip in tickets.

Portland Newspaper "Bee," February 6, 1869, earliest and best account of Blue Bucket Mine; also about Auburn by D. S. Clark, Salem, Oregon.

California Division of Mines, Ferry Bldg., San Francisco.

History of State of Idaho by Brosson.

Pioneer Days in Malheur County by J. R. Gregg.

History of Oregon Country by Scott, Vol. III, pp. 61-67, says it was 1865 before Portland population reached 6,000.

Oregon State Archives, Salem, Oregon, microfilm and files on Blue Bucket Mine.

Columbia River "I have had it" by Lyman.

Orient Meets Occident by E. A. Bryan.

Outline of Oregon's Mineral Industry by Oregon Business Review IV, No. 4, May 1945.

The Early Far West, by W. J. Ghent.

The Bonanza Trail by Muriel S. Wolle.

Oregon in the Making by Barzee, tells about old-time dances.

The Golden Land by French, tells about two routes part of the way, The Dalles to Canyon City.

Diary of Agnes Stewart, O.H.Q., Vol. 29-1928, daughter of John Stewart, member of Meek's party.

Currency Question in Oregon During Civil War by Joseph Ellison, O.H.Q., Vol. 28,-1927.

Portland Story by Thomas Prosch, O.H.Q., Vol. 14-1913.

Route of Meek's Cut-off, O.H.Q., 1934, pp. 1-9.

"Reminiscences" of Eastern Oregon by Mrs. Elizabeth Lord.

A Webfoot Volunteer by Nelson & Onstead.

O.H.Q., Vol. 16-1915, p. 133, by T. C. Elliott, tells about Bradford portage and number passengers on steamers.

Lure of the River by Fred Wilson, O.H.Q., Vol. XXX, March 1933, tells about Columbia River and hired boat builders.

"Crossing the Plains" diary, 1845, In *Willamette Farmer* issue April 18, 1879-Aug. 1, 1879.

Impressions and Observations of a Journal Man by Fred Lockley.

Notes on the Early History Grant County by H. S. Nedry, O.H.Q., LIII, Dec. 1952, pp. 236-37.

Samuel Parker's Diary, 1845, copy of file Oregon Historical Society.

History of Oregon by Bancroft, Vol. 2, "The Immigration of 1845".

Where is the Blue Bucket Mine? O.H.Q., by George H. Himes, pioneer and curator, Oregon Historical Society.

Centennial Edition Blue Mountain Eagle, Canyon City, story regarding Mr. Helms.

The Wake of the Prairie Schooner by Paden.

History Express Company, 1858, by A. L. Stimson.

History Wasco County by Wm. H. McNeal.

Samuel Parker Diary, 1845, M.S., Oregon Historical Society.

The Oregonian, Nov. 1, 1903, Blue Bucket Mine said to be identified with Canyon Creek.

Illustrated History Baker, Grant, Malheur and Harney Counties — see pg. 786 about gold hunters; also chapter VII.

History Pacific Northwest, Schafer.

Lost Emigrants of 1845 and Blue Bucket Mine (*History of Oregon Country*) by Leslie Scott.

City on the Willamette by Maddux.

Oregon Geographic Names by McArthur.

The Eastward of Cattle from the Oregon Country, story in Agricultural History XX (1946), pp. 19 43.

A Day With the Cow Column in 1843, p. 371, Oregon History 1900, by Jesse Applegate.

History of Oregon by Horace S. Lyman.

The Roads and Transportation of Territorial Oregon in Oregon Historical XL (1940), pp. 40-52.

A Brief History of the Oregon Steam Navigation Company, Oregon Historical V (1904), pp. 20-38.

Ben Holladay the Stagecoach King by J. V. Frederick.

The Mining Advance into the Inland Empire by J. Trimble, pp. 102-118.

A General History of Oregon, 1935, by Judge Charles Carey, pp. 658-710.

History of the Express Companies, 1858, by A. L. Stimson.

Centennial History of Oregon 1811-1911 by Joseph Gaston.

Pay Dirt by Quiett, pp. 170-171.

Bancroft "Scraps," p. 50.

They Built the West by Glenn Quiett.

Oregon "End of the Trail," Federal Writers project; 1st salmon cannery built 1870; by 1875 salmon pack 231,500 cases; Oregon sends cargo of wheat to Australia 1869. Most population figures come from this book.

Stage Line Portland to Sacramento, O.H.Q., Vol. 35, pp. 131-138, by Osburn Winther.

Bancroft, Vol. II, History of Oregon, p. 741, Chinaman Tax and Meek's Cut-off, p. 479; Griffin Discovering Gold, p. 479.

Pioneer Campfires by D. W. Kennedy, 1914, p. 128.

The Oregonian (Weekly), Nov. 16, 1861, story tells of the near hanging of Adams.

The Oregonian (Weekly), Aug. 31, 1861, Sept. 21, and Nov. 16, 1861 (daily); Aug. 12, 1906, all about early mining in eastern Oregon.

A Brief History of the Oregon Steam Navigation Company, O.H.Q., Vol. 5, p. 120, by P. W. Gillette, tells about freight charges, port charges.

Diary of Ralph Fisk, property of Esther Perkins, Prairie City, Oregon, tells of gold fields at Canyon City and the people; W.P.A. files.

Oregon Folks, pp. 49-61, Canyon City trail to The Dalles; also History of The Dalles, 1870, pp. 159-160.

Washington Statesman (newspaper), Walla Walla, Aug. 18, 1862, June 28, July 12, July 19, July 26, July 20 all in 1862, tells about Auburn where gold was discovered in eastern Oregon and about mining days.

Statistics of Mines and Mining West of the Rocky Mountains by R. W. Raymond, Commissioner of Mining. Serial 1424, Document 207, p. 224; Doc. 10, p. 180.

Thirty-one Years in Baker County by Isaac Hiatt, 1861-1893, says there were 151 families, 314 children, and 5,000 to 6,000 people living in Auburn early days.

East Oregonian, Pendleton, Nov. 8, 1879.

Gold by Mail, Oregonian, Sept. 14, 1865; Sept. 16, Oct. 30, 1865.

Land of Giants by David Lavender, Homestead Act, wheat; also steam boats on Columbia River.

Oregon State Constitution, Art. XV, Sec. 8, Sept. 18, 1857; also Oregon Laws 1845 to 1864, p. 815, all on tax on Chinese.

O.H.Q., Vol. 8, 1907, by F. G. Young; tax on Chinese.

O.H.Q., Vol. LX, No. 4, Post Office, information by Edward R. Payne. First post office in eastern Oregon was called Wascopum, Sept. 3, 1853; name changed to The Dalles, March 22, 1860.

Oregon Almanac, Book of facts, 1961-1962, by Social Science Division Portland State College, James E. Brooks, editor.

Land Tenure in Oregon, O.H.Q., June 1907, Vol. X, No. 2, by Lon L. Swift.

The Great Northwest by Bancroft, p. 184, production in the Willamette Valley, 1857.

Leslie Scott's History Oregon Country, Vol. 1, p. 121, says Columbia River region produced 45,000,000 bu. wheat by 1901.

U.S. Department of the Interior 22nd Annual Report to Congress, U.S. Geological Survey, June 30, 1901, by Prof. Waldemar Lindgren.

Harney County and Its Range Land by George Brimlow.

Oregon and Pacific Northwest by Lancaster Pollard, 1880, value lumber $2,030,000; by 1890 $6,530,000; by 1900 $11,080,000.

Columbia River Men in California, 1848-1849, O.H.Q., by W. M. Case, p. 169, Vol. II; tells of trading shirts to Indians for gold.

Oregon's First Monopoly the O.S.N. Co. by Irene Poppleton, O.H.Q., Vol. 9.

Oregon Times and Trails by Gene Olson.

Pacific Graveyard by James A. Gibbs, tells of the sinking of the *Brother Jonathan*.

Builders of the Northwest by Jalmar Johnson.

Oregon's Yesterdays by Fred Lockley.

Bedrock Democrat, early-day newspaper, Baker, Oregon.

R. W. Raymond, Commissioner of Mining, estimated there were 3,000 miners in eastern Oregon in 1870 averaging $8.00 per day, total $24,000 per day or about $7,200,000 a year.

Old Sumpter Newspapers – Blue Mountain American, Sumpter Miner, Sumpter Reporter, etc. Note: copies can be found at the State Geological office in Baker.

Bourne Newspaper, "The Bourne News".

Granite Newspaper, "The Granite Gem" and "The Boulder".

Greenhorn City Newspaper.

Whitney Newspaper, "The Whitney Pointer".

Baker City Chamber Commerce Report 1899, copy in the O.H.P. McCord collection, Baker.

The Oregonian, July 15, 1865, tells about gold discovery on the Burnt River.

The Oregonian, April 20, 1864, tells about the Auburn ditch.

Portland Bulletin, History Auburn, Feb. 5, 1873.

The Oregonian, June 10, July 23, 1863, story about Granite and Granite Creek.

Statistics of Mines West of the Rocky Mountains by R. W. Raymond, Doc. No. 10, Serial Congressional report No. 1811, p. 181; also Serial No. 1424, Doc. 207, p. 224.

Road South by W. S. Caverhill, former Grant County Commissioner, tells about old-time fiddlers and dances.

INDEX

* indicates a photograph

— A —

Abernathy, Governor George, 11
Adams, I. L., 32-33, 37-38
Adams Express Company, 17
Ainsworth, Captain John C., 36, 49-50*, 113
Ajax Mine, 148
Alamo (town), 148, 151
Allard, William A., 61
Althouse Creek, East Fork, 14
Althouse Creek Nugget, 16
Ankeny, Captain A. P., 22, 54, 99
Ankeny, Levi, 99
Applegate, Jesse, 10, 12*
Applegate, Lindsay, 10, 12*
Applegate Trail, 11, 12
Arlington Hotel, 97
Armstrong, George, 113
Armstrong Nugget, 76, 113*
Arrastra: horse-powered, 29*; water-powered, 77*, 111*, 142*
Astoria, 9
Auburn (town), 39-41, 40*, 49, 59, 95
Auburn Canal Company, 95
Auburn Ditch, 95, 112
Auburn Water Company, 95
Austin, Minot and Linda, 133, 136*
Austin, 133, 136, 137*

— B —

Badger Mine, 75, 76*
Baisley-Elkhorn Mine, 110*, 143
Bakeoven (town), 59*
Baker, Colonel Edward, 95
Baker (town), 38-39, 41, 95-101, 96*, 100*, 101*, 104
Baker-Canyon stage, 65*
Baker City. See: Baker
Baker Concert Band, 107*
Baker Hotel, 102
Bancroft, Hubert Howe, 6
B & H Company, 166
Bank of Sumpter, 123*, 128*
Bannock War, 59
Baring, Alexander, 138, 163
Barlow, Samuel Kimbrough, 10
Barlow toll road, 42
Barlow Trail, 9
Barry-Way, Jim. See: Berriway
Bartlett, Ed., 91*
P. Basche Store, 101*
Bates (town), 133

Becker, Charles, 61
Bedrock Democrat (newspaper), 46, 97
Beekman, C. C., 17, 19*
Belshaw, Charles, 65
Ben Harrison Mine, 144, 148
Berriway, Jim, 59
Bi Metallic Mine, 93*, 144
Big Johnny Mine, 93*
Black Hawk Mine, 78, 83*
Black Pine Mine, 146*
Blaine Mine, 148
Bloch-Miller and Company, 44
Blue Bird Mine, 108*
Blue Mountains, 138, 158
Blue Mountain American (newspaper), 41, 118, 140
Blue Mountain Eagle (newspaper), 46, 68
Blue Mountain Times (newspaper), 56
Blue Ribbon Mine, 148
Bonanza Hoisting Plant, 134*
Bonanza Mine, 78, 113, 132, 134*-135*, 143, 163
Bonanza Saloon, 129
Bourne, Jonathan Jr., 138
Bourne (town), 138, 140*, 160, 164
Bradford, B. F., 49
Briggs, David, 27*
Briggs Pocket Mine, 27
Britt, Peter, 20
Bromberg, Erick, 24
Brother Jonathan (steamer), 31, 37*
Brown, A. H., 97, 104
Brown, Ben, 56
Buck Creek placers, 76
Buffalo Mine, 144, 148
Buncom (town), 24
Bunker Hill Mine, 138, 140
Burnt River, 38
Burnt River Bridge and Ferry Company, 106
Butler, Bob, 79
Butterfield Overland Stage, 30

— C —

Cabell Mine, 75
Caldwell, S. A., 113
California Mine, 144
Canyon City, 6-7, 31, 53, 57, 59, 61, 63*, 66, 68-69
Canyon City (fire), 60*
Canyon City Museum, 86

Canyon Creek, 6-7, 11, 61
Capitol Hotel, 126
Carson, M. C., 93*
Carter, George C., 131
Cascade Locks, 49, 51*
Cascade portage. See: Cascade Locks
Cayuse War, 8
Chambers, Sarah, 6
Chief Buffalo Horn, 59
Chief Egan, 59
Chief Paulina, 57
Chinese, in Southern Oregon, 24-25
Chinese gold scales, 25*
    mining shovel, 41*
    opium smoker, 71*
City Journal, 63
City of Sumpter (dredge boat), 126
Claggage, Jim, 13
Clark, J. W., 91*
Clarksville, 104
Clayton, George, 44
Clough, E. E., 109
Club Saloon, 129
Cobb, C. B., 69
Coe, I. W., 49
Cohn, E. B., 109
Cola, Bill, 92
Columbia Mine, 138, 140*-141*
Columbia Press. See: Umatilla Press
Columbia River, 4, 7-10
Comer, R. H. J., 63-64
Comer (town), 73
Concord Mine, 143, 148
Congo Mine, 148
Congregational Church, 67*
Connor Creek Mine, 115*
Contest Rock, 91*, 92
Continental Mine, 148
Coos Bay, 13
Copeland, J. W., 129
Copia mines. See: Cornucopia Mines
Coquille River, 24
Cornelius, Thomas R., 6-7
Cornucopia Mine, 152-153*, 154-155*, 157, 166
Cornucopia (town), 153-155
Couch, Captain John, 32
Cougar Mine, 144, 148-149*
"Cousin-Jacks," 152, 154
Cracker City. See: Bourne
Cracker Creek, 138
Cracker-Eagle Gold Mine, 141*
Craig, Austin, 129
Cranston, Ed, 39
Crosby, Captain Nathaniel, 32, 34

— D —

Daggett, William, 78, 113
Dalles, The, story, 42-48
Davis, W. M., 73
De Bilk, Madam, 44
De Roo, P., 97
Decker General Store, 14-15*
Diadem Mine, 93*
Dickerson Mine, 150*
Dickson Mine, 116
Ditmars, J. N., 147
Dixie Meadows Mine, 73*
Dixie Town, 73
Dockery, Jack, 91*
Dolling, George, 73
Don Juan Mine, 78-79*
Donation Act of 1850, 16-17
"doodlebug" washing plants, 126, 127*
Dooley, Jere, 104
Downie Mine, 116, 122
Draper, William F., 89
Dredge boat, 27
Dredge buckets, 127*
Dredge mining, 126
Dryer, T. J., 33
Dunn, Dan, 92
Durbin, John, 6

— E —

Eagleton, Tom, 147
E & E Mine, 138
Easterly Mine, 17*
Eccles, David, 99, 129
Eldorado Ditch, 104, 107, 112
Elk Creek, 74
Elk Creek placers, 75*
Elkhorn Hotel, 68*
Elliott, David, 79
Elliott, Mrs. Johanna, 79*
Elliott, Mr. Otis J., 79*
Ellis Mine, 116, 122
Estabrook, G. W., 109
Eureka & Excelsior (quartz mine), 138

— F —

Farmer House (hotel), 36, 43*
Fearing, E. B., 69
Ferris Mining Company, 166
Fields, Walter, 68
Fields Diary, 4
First Methodist Church, 33
First National Bank of Baker City, 99
First National Bank gold exhibit,
    104-105* (Baker, Oregon)
Flagstaff Mine, 104
Ford, Otis, 147
Forest Creek, 24
Fort Boise, 3, 5*
Fort Dalles, 42
Fort Hall, Idaho, 3, 4*-5, 10
Fort Sumter. See: Sumpter
Fort Walla Walla, 8*, 38, 54
Forty-ninth Parallel, 11
Franklin House (hotel), 36
Fraser, Thomas, 33
Fredrick, Mr., 91*
French Pete, 39

Fretag, Louis E., 107
Furguson, James F., 98*

— G —

Galice, Dr. Louis, 25*
Galliger, John, 59
Gavin, "49 Jimmy," 78, 80*
Geiser, Albert, 100, 132, 163
Geiser (town), 131-133*
Geiser Grand Hotel, 100*-101, 103*
Gem Mine, 110*
Gem Saloon, 118, 123*, 129
General Lane (ship), 12
Gillette, P. W., 54
Gilliam, Albert, 144
Gilliland, Verna, 83*
Gimlet Creek, 113
Gin Lin, 24*
Globe Hotel, 44*
Golconda Mine, 138, 140
Gold:
    largest nugget, 14
    map of mines, 72
    mining stocks, 158*, 164*
    nuggets, 6*, 62*, 112*-113*, 114*
    panning, 26*, 167*
    picks (homemade), 41*
    production, California Mines Report
        #58, 168-169
    production records by U.S. Govern-
        ment, 168-169
    scales, 63*, 106*
    shipments by ocean steamers and ex-
        press, 60
    slugs, 165*, 166
    sponge, 156*
Gold, discovered:
    in California, 11
    in eastern Oregon (Griffin Gulch),
        37-38
    in southern Oregon, 1850, 13
Gold Coin Mine, 78
Gold Hill Mine, 26-27*
Golden Eagle Mine, 78, 86*
Golden Gate Mine, 78, 85*
Graham, Billy, 143
Grand Hotel, 146*-147
Grande Ronde Sentinel (newspaper), 56
Granite (town), 144-148
Granite Gem (paper), 147
Grant County, 61, 68
Grant County Museum, 31, 59, 63*, 65
Grants Pass, Oregon, 10
Graves Creek, 11
Great Northern Mine, 75*
Green-Horn Mountains, 76-78, 81
Greenback Mine, 28*
Greenhorn (town), 81, 84*, 86-87*, 89-90,
    92
Greenhorn Investigator (newspaper), 89
Greenhorn placers, 115
Greenhorn Townsite Patent, 84*
Grier and Kellogg Livery Stable, 101,
    102*
Griffin, Henry, 37-38, 41
Griffin Gulch, 38
Griffin Hotel, 122
Griggs, George, 109
Gutridge, Al, 92

— H —

Haggard, Jack, 132, 134
Haight, Clinton P., 73
Hall, George Washington, 39-40*
Hall Hotel, 138
Handley, Dan, 47
Hard rock mining, 29*
Hardy, Mrs. Maggie, 89
Harkerader brothers, 109
Harvest Queen, The (boat), 57*
Hassalo, The (riverboat), 52*
Hay, Dr. Ing, 69, 71
Hayes, President Rutherford B., 17
Hazeltine, George I., 64*-65, 69
Heilner, W. H., 109
Helm, William F., 6-7
Hendryx, H. E., 148
Henley, Leone, 85
Henley, Marcus, 91*
Herberger, John, 61, 65
Herren, Don, 6-7
Hidden Treasure (quartz mine), 82
Himes, George H., 6
Hogum. See: Sanger
Holden, M., 89
Holladay, Ben, 106
Homestead Act, 1862, 54
Honolulu (schooner), 11
Hornicker, August, 91*
Howard, James, 148
Hoyt, George W., 49
Hudson's Bay Company, 3-5, 8, 10, 13,
    16, 42
Hull, Frank G., 148
Humason, Orlando, 38
Humbolt Drive, 61
Humbolt Mine, 78, 83*
Hyde, H. H., 73

— I —

Ibex Mine, 138
Illinois River, 13-14
Imperial Mine, 144
Independence Mine, 144, 148
Index map: (placer & gold mines), 22*
Indian uprising, Columbia River, 1855, 8
Intrinsic Mine. See: Bi Metallic Mine
I.X.L. mine, 78, 82*

— J —

Jackson, M. S., 89
Jackson County, 14, 17
Jacksonville (town), 13-14*, 16-21, 24, 26
Jewett Mine, 26
John Day, 6, 66, 69-70*
John Day River, 4, 7, 61
Johnson, Oscar, 100*
Johnson, William, 32
Jollison, Mrs. J. A., 129
Josephine County, 14
Judy, Lloyd, 148

— K —

Kam Wah Chung Company, 69, 71*
Kane, William, 31
Kelley, William H., 89

Kelly, Fred J., 82*
Kerbyville (Kerby), 16, 24
King, A. W., 129
King, Colonel William, 33
Knickerbocker Trust Company, 164
Krause, Mr. & Mrs. Walter, 85*

— L —

La Bellevue Mine, 148-149*
La Dalle. See: The Dalles
La Grande, 56
Ladd, William S., 49
Lane, Joseph, 11-12
Larson, Andy, 89, 91*
Last Chance Mine, 152, 157
Lawton (town), 148, 151*
Lawton Standard (paper), 148
Le Brent, Jules, 73
Leiken Brothers, 109
Lemon, Ira, 89, 92
Lewis and Clark, 42
Lewis Investment Company, 166
Libbey, F. W., 168
"Lincoln Skins," 31
Lindgren, Professor J. Waldemar, 61,
   106, 157, 169
Liston Mine, 91
Littlefield, David, 37, 38*
Llano de Oro. See: Easterly Mine
Lockley, Fred, 19, 42
Long Creek Eagle (newspaper), 81
"Lost Blue Bucket Mine," 6-8, 38
Lost Wagontrain of 1845, 4*, 6
Lovejoy, A. L., 32
Lower Town. See: John Day
Lownsdale, Daniel H., 32
Luelling and Meek, Nurserymen, 30
Lung On, 69

— Mc —

McBean, Frank, 75*
McCall, Harold, 83
McCord, O. H. P., 97-98*
McCord, Robert, 98
McCord, S. B., 97-98
McCord Blacksmith Shop & Foundry, 97
McCoy, Fred, 148
McCrary, William, 95
McCullum, Frank I., 69
McEwen, Tom, 138, 163
McNamee Gulch, 113
McNemee, Emaline, 6
McNemee, Job, 32
McWillis Gulch placer, 89*

— M —

Magnolia Mine, 148
Malheur City, 104, 106-107*
Malheur River, 4, 6
Mallory, Franklin, 104
Mammoth Mines and Mill, 140*
Marshall, Jack, 91
Martin, H. D., 6
Massamore, George W., 87, 89
Meek, Joseph L., 3-4, 11
Meek, Stephen H., 3-4*
Meek Party, 4, 6-8

Mercury flask, 41*
Middlesworth, P. V., 69
Midway Mine, 121*
Millard, J. E., 89
Miller, Burton, 81
Miller, Joaquin. See: Miller, Cincin-
   natus Hiner
Miller, Cincinnatus Hiner, 64-66, 89
Miller and Draper (store), 93
Mine drilling, 28*
Miner's candlesticks, 151*
Mint at The Dalles, 46
Mint Saloon, 129
Monarch Mine, 148
Monumental Mine, 144, 148
Mormon Special. See: Sumpter Valley
   Railroad
Morning Democrat, 78
Morning Glory Mine, 78
Morrison Bridge, 36
Mosier, Shorty, 69
Mount Hood Saloon, 47
Mountain Slide Mine, 30*
Mountaineer (newspaper), 46*
Mud wagon, 58*
Mullen, Mr. & Mrs. Bill, 90
Mullen, Mrs. Kate, 86
Mullen, Mr. & Mrs. Vic, 89
Multnomah County, 33
Murphy-Murray dredge, 27*
Myers, Ray, 83, 86
Myrick, Josiah, 49

— N —

Nelson placers, 115
New Market Theater, 22, 23*
New York (hotel), 36
Nokes, Nick, 137*
North Pole Mine, 138, 139*
Northwest-Development Company, 166
Nugget Saloon, 147*

— O —

O'Bryant, Hugh D., 33
O'Dair, J. J., 147
O'Farrel, Mollie, 129
Ohio House, 32
Okanagan (steamer), 54
Old Dry (claim), 109
Old Greenhorn, 81
Oliver, Joe C., 65, 68
Olney, Nathan, 3
Ore-Bin, 168-69
Ore car, 151*
Oregon:
   became a state, 1859, 30
   declared a territory, 1848, 11
Oregon City, 7, 9-10, 36
Ocsgon Historical Quarterly, 24, 54
Oregon Historical Society, 6
The Oregon Journal (newspaper), 19
Oregon Lumber Company, 99, 129,
   132*-133
Oregon Mining Journal, 157
Oregon Mining Review, 148, 169
Oregon Portage Railroad, 50*
Oregon Smelting & Refining Company,
   120*, 130*
Oregon Spectator (newspaper), 7*, 19

Oregon Steam Navigation Company, 36,
   43*, 49-50, 54
Oregon Trail, 8, 10, 17, 38, 42, 95
Oregonian (paper), 33 -34*, 107, 137
O.S.N. See: Oregon Steam Navigation
   Company
Overland Stage, 37
   stage schedule, 21*
Overton, William, 32
Owl Mine, 78

— P —

Packhurst, Charlie, 21*
Packwood, Augusta, 112
Packwood, William H., 39-40*, 95, 107,
   109
Palmer, J., 54
Patch, Sanford, 6
Parrish, Hon. Charles W., 61, 63*
Parrish, Philip H., 168
Patterson, Orin S., 68
Peart, William, 89
Pete Mann Ditch Company, 112*
Pettygrove, Francis W., 32
Phoenix Mine, 78-80*
Pioneer Stage Line, 106
Pittsburgh Mining Company, 132
Placer miner's experience, 77*
Polk, President James K., 11
Pollard, Lancaster, 49
Pomeroy Dredge, 75*
Pony, The (steam engine), 49
Poole, James R., 13
"poor man's mining," 28
Portage Railroad, 52*
Porter and Company, 166
Portland, 9, 12, 32-36, 49
Portland harbor, 35*-36*
Powell, Theophilus, 7
Prairie City, 73
Prairie City Miner (newspaper), 73
Prairie Diggings, 64, 69
Prairie Diggins Mine, 71*
Psyche Mine, 93*
Pyx Mine, 78, 85*

— Q —

Queen of the West (quartz mine), 152

— R —

Rabbit Mine, 78
Raymond, Rossiter W., 61, 169
Raymond Hotel, 140*
Red Bird Mine, 78
Red Boy Mine, 142*-144, 148
Red Jacket Mine, 152
Red Lion Hotel, 86-87*, 90-91
Red Lion Saloon, 91*
Reed, Simeon C., 33, 49
Rich Gulch, 13
Richardson, Simeon Childs, 81, 84-86
Roaring Gimlet Mine, 26
Robbins, Harvey, 144-145
Robbins, J. H., 143
Robinson, William, 78
Robinsonville, 78, 80-81
Rock-drilling contests, 91-92

Rocky Mountain Canaries, 14*
Rogers, Bert, 89, 92
Rogers, Sam, 97
Rogue River, 13
Rogue River camps: 16
    Pleasant Creek, Evans Creek, Willow
    Creek, Foots Creek, Starvout,
    Jumpoff Joe, Coyote, Graves, Tom
    East Creek.
Rogue River system: 16
    Kerbyville, Williams Creek, Althouse
    Creek, Applegate River
Roseburg, Oregon, 10
Ross, William W., 109
Royal White Mine, 78, 86*
Ruckel, Colonel J. S., 95-96, 104
Rust, Henry, 101-102

— S —

Sailors Diggings. See: Decker General
    Store
St. Clair, Mary, 47
St. Thomas Episcopal Church, 65*, 68
Sampson Company, Ltd., 138, 160-162
Samuel Roberts (schooner), 13
San Francisco mint, 59
Sanger, 109-110
Sanger Ditch, 112
Sanger Mine, 110-112*
Saunders, S. B., 129
Schneider, Chris, 154, 157
Schriver, F. W., 37-38
Scott, Levi, 13
Scottsburg, 13, 15*-16
Sells, H. L., 64*-65, 71
Seufert, Frank, 45
Shanghai Gulch (placer), 109-110
Shanghai-Moultrie Mine, 109
Shearer, Joe, 57
Shearers Bridge, 57*
Shively, J. M., 9
The Sierra Nevada (ship), 59*
Simmons, Lon, 152
Simpson, Isaac, 6-7
Sinnott, Nick, 47
16-to-1 Mine, 97*
Sluice boxes, 26*
Smith, Thomas, 33
Snake River, 3-5
Snow Creek Mine, 94*
Southern Oregon Historical Museum,
    18*
Spanish Tom, 39
Sparta, 109
Sparta Stage, 110*
Stafford, William, 37-38
Stamp mill, 111*
Stark, Benjamin, 49
Stearns, D. H., 113
Stephens, James B., 36
Sterling Creek, 22, 24
Sterling Mine, 22, 23*
Sterlingville, 24
Stevenson, E. G., 81, 84-85*, 89, 91*
Stevenson, Harry, 79
Steward, Frank, 79
Steward, Pearl, 79
Steward, William, 79

Steward, Mrs. William, 85*
Stewart, Henry, 148
Stices Gulch placer, 114*
Stott, Sam R., 89
Stump Dodger. See: Sumpter Valley
    Railroad
"Stump Town." See: Portland
Sumpter, 92, 116-118, 122, 124*-126
The Sumpter Miner (paper), 115
Sumpter News, 78, 116, 118, 140
Sumpter Smelter, 116
Sumpter Valley:
    dredge boat, 126*
    freight train, 130*
    passenger train, 132*, 137*
Sumpter Valley Dredging Company, 166
Sumpter Valley Hotel, 129
Sumpter Valley Railroad, 99, 116,
    129-132, 137
Susanville, 74-75

— T —

Table Rock Sentinel (newspaper), 17, 19
Tabor Fraction Mine, 138, 140
Taft, President Wm. Howard, 84
Takelma (town and area), 19
Tenino (steamer), 53*-54
Terwilliger, James, 6-7, 32
Tetherow, Solomon, 6
The Clearing, 32
The Dalles (town), 4-10, 31, 42-43*,
    46*-47, 53, 57, 59
The Dalles City (steamer), 55*
The Dalles Journal, 46
The Landing. See: The Dalles.
The Whitney (hotel), 129
Thomas, Lelia, 129
Thompson, ex-Governor David P., 22
Thompson, Riley, 129
Thompson, Robert R., 49
Thornburg, Grant, 145-147
Tiger Town. See: John Day
Times-Mountaineer, 45
Timms Gold Dredging Company, 166
Tipton (town), 132-133, 137*
Totten, John, 131
Town Mine, 26
Trevitt, Vic, 47
Trowbridge, B. C., 64*-65
Tualatin plains, 12
Turner, Bill, 151
T'Vault, William G., 6-7, 17, 19*

— U —

Umatilla House, 44, 47*-48*, 53
Umatilla Landing, 54-46*
Umatilla Press (newspaper), 56
Umpqua River, 13, 15*
Umpqua Weekly Gazette (newspaper),
    16
Union-Companion Mine, 152-153*
Union Pacific, 118
Upper Town. See: Canyon City
United States Hotel, 17
U.S. Mint, 30, 46

— V —

Vale, 4
Vinegar Butte, 76-77*, 81
Virginian Mine, 78-79*
Virtue, J. W., 104, 109, 113
Virtue Bank, 97-98*
Virtue Mine, 95, 104, 106*

— W —

Wage scale (Sumpter, Oregon, 1903),
    121*
Waiilatpu, 11
Waldo, 14, 16*
Wallula (port), 50
War Production Boards' Administrative
    Order L-208, 28, 157, 166
Warren, Jim, 87, 89-91, 129
Warshauer Hotel. See: Geiser Grand
    Hotel
Wasco County, 31, 42
Wasco-Pum. See: The Dalles
Wells Fargo Express Company, 17, 57,
    60*, 97
Wey, Berry, 58*
Wheeler, Henry, 57
Whiskey Gulch, 61
Whiskey Run, 24
White, F. Wallace, 138, 160-164
White Swan Band. See: Baker Concert
    Band
White Swan Mine, 104, 107*
Whitman Massacre, 8
Whitman Mission, 11
Whitney (town), 129, 131
Whitney Forwarding Company, 131
Wiegand, Alice, 89
Wiegand, George R., 89
Willamette Falls. See: Oregon City
Willamette Valley, 3, 8-11, 13-14
Williams, Richard, 49
Wilson, G. H., 89
Winchester, 13
Win-Quatt. See: The Dalles
Wisdom, Jefferson D., 88*-89
Wolf Creek (placer mine), 31*
Wolverine Jack, 93*
Wood-burning engine, 133*
Woodwell, A. H., 126-127*
Wool, General John Ellis, 8
Worley Mine, 78, 115
Wyeth, Nathaniel, 4

— Y —

Young, Joseph D., 116
Yreka, 13

— Z —

Zimmerman, Peter, 61